BOOK & BABY

The Complete Guide
to Managing *Chaos*
& Becoming
a Wildly Successful
Writer-Parent

BY MILDA M. DEVOE
FOUNDER OF PEN PARENTIS

BROOKLYN
WRITERS PRESS

Published in New York City by the Brooklyn Writers Press,
an imprint of the Brooklyn Writers Co. LLC.

www.brooklynwriterspress.com

TITLE: Book & Baby, The Complete Guide to Managing Chaos & Becoming A Wildly Successful Writer-Parent

ISBN: 978-1-952991-06-6 (e-book)
ISBN: 978-1-952991-07-3 (paperback)

Library of Congress Catalog Card Number: 2020922340

1st Edition

AUTHOR WEBSITE: mmdevoe.com

To every writer who has kids,
may you follow your creative passions

CONTENTS

PART 3: WRITING WITH A TODDLER

PART 4: WRITING WITH A LITTLE KID

PART 5: WRITING WITH A BIG KID

PART 6: WRITING WITH A TEEN

PART 7: WRITING WITH AN EMPTY NEST

THE WRITER'S SNACK JAR: EXTRA CONTENT FOR THE HUNGRY WRITER

INTRODUCING YOUR NARRATOR

M. M. DeVoe

Hello.

Never did I ever think I was going to start a nonprofit. Or get married. Or of all things, become a mother. My journey to founding Pen Parentis is as randomly roving as a book by Proust. Yet here I am, an award-winning writer with two children, married over 25 years, and happily running a successful organization that helps keep writers on creative track after they start a family.

In writing circles, there's a dichotomy between "Planners" who outline their plots and then fill in the details to get to the end, and "Pantsers" who start writing and end up wherever their imaginations take them—plotting by the seat of their pants.

**In writing, I'm a "Pantser" and it turns out,
in life I'm a "Pantser" too.**

As a child, I was a performer. I was the kid who organized skits at holiday gatherings, who got my three younger brothers and three younger cousins and sometimes my two neighbors together with finger puppets, or marionettes, or just the soundtrack of a musical or a movie and ourselves, and who created stories and dramas for all of us to act out. There were variety shows in the driveway, sing-alongs on my grandmother's stairwell, Martha Graham-style dance numbers with ribbons or balls or long scarves on the lawn in Texas—these often interrupted by someone stepping on a sticker in their bare feet. (Stickers are vicious ground-growing weeds that culminate in seeds that are basically a pea-sized hard round ball with dozens of sharp spikes. They'll penetrate any callus, and god forbid you fall over in a patch of them.) Our earliest audiences were always adults, sometimes appreciative, usually full of constructive criticism: "That's nice, but maybe you could practice some more. What are those terrible lyrics? Is this even appropriate for kids? Why are you using my power drill as a prop?"

> **Compared to stepping on a sticker,**
> **no amount of artistic criticism is painful.**
> **It's all just words.**

I loved the applause. I sang all the time: around the house, in the shower, at the side of the road waiting for the school bus. By the time I was nine, I was sure I would be a world-famous opera singer who was as smart as Sabrina from Charlie's Angels and looked like Cher. I started entering talent shows. In third grade I floored my elementary school teachers by belting out Helen Reddy's "I am Woman, Hear Me Roar" to a standing ovation. At home, my mother told me I was never to sing another song like that.

To this day, I don't know what she meant. Feminist? Powerful? Was it my high-heels and sparkly pantsuit, borrowed from a friend? Or was it the pop-star quality of basking in the attention of strangers she was objecting to?

I kept singing. I joined choirs. Church choir, middle school musical, high school choir... I played the lead in every musical, the supporting comedic character on alternate nights. I loved to perform. I signed up for drama, jazz and ballet classes at our local community center. I played the piano, took voice lessons, and briefly attempted the guitar until the F-chord gently showed me that this instrument hated me. I loved the immediate response of performance: when I did great; it garnered applause. When I messed up, that was equally clear. Performing live taught me that every audience wants you to succeed—and even when you fail, they expect you to dust yourself off and keep at it. Live performance taught me grit.

When I was fifteen, they sent me for two years to a Lithuanian boarding school in Germany. To understand this random event, know that I was born to Lithuanian DPs (displaced persons). Both my father and mother had parents who escaped the Soviet occupation of their homeland. In today's parlance, my parents were "Dreamers." After coming of age in different Chicago Lithuanian immigrant neighborhoods (yes, there were two of them!), my parents met, married, and moved to Texas to escape the 1966-70 race rioting in Chicago's South Side—at the time my parents were young, forward-looking, college-educated adults who believed passionately in Civil Rights and equality for all, but not in bloodshed for any reason. I was their first child and raised bilingual, with a strong sense of Lithuanian identity in the middle of Texas, taught to represent my parents' homeland, so in my childhood, I spent an inordinate amount of time wearing a Lithuanian folk costume and explaining the mushroom or potato-based foods that I was handing out for sampling—not just during the annual "Heritage Days" at school but also during "International Day" at the local shopping mall. Potlucks at church or school always meant we had to educate our neighbors on Lithuanian cooking. Culture through food.

During the Soviet Era, West Germany boasted of the only Lithuanian High School in the free world. Lithuanian parents from all over the world sent their kids there for at least a year (mine begged some nuns to give their kid a scholarship) and I and other "displaced" Lithuanians, aka DPs learned the language, history, and literature of a country that the Soviet Union forcibly occupied after the Second World War. We were told we needed to keep the culture alive because in the Soviet Union, even praying in the native language was illegal. We were told that strict Roman Catholicism was patriotic. Folk dancing in costume was a political demonstration. Folk songs were subversive, and many had hidden or double meanings.

Outside of my family, I knew no other Lithuanians who could tell me whether any of this was true, but I believed it.

There were Lithuanian families like mine all over Texas, but back then I was craving community so desperately I once wrote a letter to a complete stranger whose first and last names were Lithuanian. I found this person I wanted to befriend randomly in a Houston phone book and pleaded and begged them to write back. They never did.

This cultural indoctrination was important to my parents. We were not wealthy: they raised my three younger brothers and me in the country outside of a small college town where my father had the salary of a postdoc chemistry researcher for most of his life. My mother ran a tiny Montessori school that never charged more than the bare minimum, because she believed all children deserved a great preschool education (she would have run that school for free if someone had donated the requisite pink tower and maps and covered the expenses of feeding the school's geese and occasionally painting or exterminating the fire ants in the schoolyard). I survived overseas for two years on a $50 per month allowance, and that, to me, seemed generous since our food bill for six people, three of whom were active growing boys, was $100 per week—which again seemed like an enormous expense that the family was always trying to cut.

Money was always an issue, but one that I could grow beyond. I learned to find free events to attend, to take advantage of opportunities, to recycle, to be thrifty. I learned to make do with what I had, and to shop around for bargains. I learned that style was less expensive than fashion — and more valuable in the long run. I learned that experiences were longer-lasting and more transformative than objects, and that ideas cost nothing and could change everything. It was an important period in my life.

After my two years in boarding school, I returned to the United States fluent in both Lithuanian and German, and I entered college as a fiercely activist anti-Soviet music major. I attended a tiny Catholic women's college in Baltimore, brilliantly named the College of Notre Dame of Maryland. They have since changed the name, but oh what a delicious acronym to toss around ironically while I was a student! The college's chief strength was that they, as a nun-driven school, were feminist and appreciative of young women's inner fortitude and personal drive (if you know any nuns in person you will understand this) and gave us free rein and lots of administrative support to do whatever it was we wanted to do. You just had to find the rules that gave you the permission. As Freshman class president, I learned that heavy bureaucracy could either drive you up a wall, or (if you could keep your head), you could learn to check off the infinite boxes and get whatever you need. Dealing with a bureaucratic Catholic school system would serve me well when I eventually applied for government grants.

This time period was also where I learned about grassroots marketing. There were layers of flyers for contests, free events, and job offers posted on the bulletin boards at school–if you blew by them without reading, you'd never know what was going on. I was the kid who attended all the free events thrown by the Student Activities Committee–often the only student in the audience not required to attend; I could meet all the folk singers, authors, comedians, motivational speakers, etc., that came through the college. I learned a lot from these one-on-one conversations with professional entrepreneurs in the performing arts. They were scrappy. They would play an empty room for money. They would use photographs and memorabilia to turn a disastrous performance into a fabulous newspaper article or interview that made them look great. They were marketing before marketing was even a major.

In my junior year of college, I also won my first national writing contest. Remember, I am not from a wealthy background. My three younger brothers all needed to attend the Lithuanian boarding school for at least a year. This was my parents' priority: College was on me to fund. My parents could cover my textbooks, but even that was a hardship. On a full academic scholarship that included room and board, I attended a four-year college, but I still had to come up with my own pocket money. Since international travel was high on my list of To-Dos, and credit card offers had been pouring into my mailbox from the minute I first opened a bank account, I was already $900 in debt by my junior year. To a college student, this was a desperate, impossible amount, even though I was earning $6/hour at a "great" part-time job in a fitness center. Imagine my delight to find a college poetry contest with a top prize of $1000 thumb tacked to the English Department's cluttered board.

I submitted a villanelle I had written for my prosody class, and to my great delight, I won the grand prize.

Not only did this create a little rocklike seed of faith in my writing talent, it made me believe in the power of a thumb tacked flyer. I submitted further poetry to various other contests, always things I had written for class. While I had always adored languages (I had by then added classes in Spanish and Italian to my Lithuanian and German), this was the first time I realized that I was not a bad wordsmith, even in my native tongue!

I was a busy kid in college. Not only did I dance in a Lithuanian folk dance troupe and attend political demonstrations in Washington DC nearly every weekend, but also, on campus, I started a drama club, directed a musical, founded a singing telegram company, and revived three old College traditions (Sing-Song, the faculty talent show, and a candlelit Ivy Walk to sing to the seniors). I would discover a need in the community (or in myself!) and then just start making things happen. It was an active time–filled with passionate late-night arguments about politics, creativity, and the arts. I knew what I wanted in life and driven to get it.

And in junior year, after winning that contest, I felt the limitless possibilities of choice. Debt-free at last, I took a background role in a John Waters movie, and when it wrapped, I ran away with a troupe of jugglers for a summer, and they became my best friends for life. I had vague ideas of a glamorous future: I would either join an opera company and tour the world, or I would get a job in the Lithuanian consulate and train to become an ambassador. Meanwhile, I was taking 19-23 credits per semester, performing and dating half the people who attended Johns Hopkins, Loyola, and the Naval Academy in Annapolis, all while staying on the Dean's List.

I didn't realize this was unusual.

And then in March of my senior year in College, Lithuania declared its independence from the Soviet Union. My friends and I, globally, had succeeded. Lithuania was free. I no longer needed to attend demonstrations, folk-dancing got downgraded from a political event to a charming if slightly odd little hobby, and even my fluency in this difficult foreign language was suddenly archaic and bizarre instead of brave and fiercely patriotic. All of this happened overnight. I lost my core identity in one newspaper headline. I was no longer a freedom-fighter.

I was nothing: just a girl who had been born in a small town in Texas and called herself Lithuanian.

But I still had my singing. I still had performance. I still got applause.

What I didn't have was any career guidance.

The Music Department faculty consisting of two excellent pianists, an adorable but dotty nun who directed the choir, a part-time flautist and a part-time voice teacher who was best known for playing the lead in "The Bird Cage" at a local dinner theater. They were all loving and nurturing of talent, but they were not managers. I knew I loved performance, but after college, what did artists do to get jobs? I had no idea. No one told me there was such a thing as a graduate school for opera, so I auditioned for something I saw on a flyer and got into an acting school called AMDA–the American Musical and Dramatic Academy in New York City. It started three days after my twenty-first birthday, which coincidentally was also my college graduation day.

So that's what I did. I moved to New York City and found I was home.

HOW TO USE THIS BOOK

Ladies and gentlemen and sweet writers of nonbinary persuasion: This book is a guide.

Think of it as a doula for your writing project. Writing is a 24/7 career. Parenting is a 24/7 responsibility. Reading is... a break from all that. This book is here to help, not to pile on to your already massive load of guilt for unfinished projects! If you are a parent, you definitely have massive loads of laundry, or dishes, or homework help, or hopefully writing or editing to do, and you definitely don't have time to read this book cover to cover.

The good news is, there is no wrong way to read this book.

There are sections organized by the age of the child which will address the resources of time, energy and money. You could read the entire book in small chunks. Read only those sections that affect you personally. Skip around. Go where your heart leads you. Keep it by your bedside for inspiration. Glance at it when you feel down.

Need inspiration? Jump to a story from the salons.

Need to know what's coming next?

Page forward to the part about writing with older kids.

Feeling jealous that someone else won the Pulitzer this year? If they appear in this book (and there's a good chance they might!) just look up their interview and recognize that they also struggled, they made sacrifices; they weren't sure what they were doing, they persevered, they finished their writing project, and you can too.

STORIES FROM THE SALONS

DeVoe with Kelly Link, April 2013

Interspersed throughout this book, you will find interviews with notable writers who are parents. Let their very different opinions and solutions liberate you to discover your own solutions. Just as you do when you go to a library–read the books that inspire you, feed you. Dismiss the words that feel wrong. When you read a book, you are not reading to copy the writing word for word, you're reading to feel something—even if it's just a need to escape! Do that with these interviews. They are real stories that happened to real people who publish and win prizes and make something of their literary careers. Let their stories wash over you and fill you with possibility. Whatever you choose to do will be right for you and your family. If it isn't, guess what? You can change it.

THE SNACK JAR

At the end, we have assembled a collection of fun facts, interesting comments, and various other tidbits that will interest writers who are also parents. Visit the Snack Jar whenever you feel the need to feed your writing soul!

Let's summarize this entire book in the three words: YOU CAN TOO.

You don't have to.

There is no right path to follow.

This won't be easy.

(At all.)

But you can.

And if you do, it's worth it.

PART 1

The Impossible Conundrum

BECOMING A WRITER

I loved NYC with all my heart. While I felt empty from the lack of international politics, no longer was it weird that I was Lithuanian. Most people I met had vaguely heard of the country, or at least that the Soviet Union had broken up. Politics was acceptable cocktail party conversation here, and so was culture. And being an avid reader helped. I spent two years working hard on character voices and learning a musical theater repertoire. I'd had no formal training in drama and here's how naïve I was: at my first monologue audition instead of facing the judges, I pretended there was an invisible person on stage with me and played the monologue to her. The judges giggled until one kind soul gently told me to place my invisible partner in the back row of the audience.

My last year of acting school, disaster struck. I developed vocal nodes from the late nights, lack of nutrition, and endless loud and lunatic character roles. With a lack of actual income and no medical insurance, all I do was go on six weeks of vocal rest. My friends were auditioning for world tours and cruise ships, and I was writing responses on a small notebook like a mute person. My new boyfriend was supportive and kind, and though we practically lived together and did in actuality work together, despite the intimacy of existing 24/7 in each other's company, I wasn't comfortable letting him in on my financial situation (destitute with no prospects), so he couldn't help. I never dreamed I would end up marrying the guy. I never dreamed I would marry anyone.

Once my nodes went away, I discovered I had permanently damaged my vocal cords and probably could not sing professionally. Once again, I had to reinvent myself. Instead of the musical theater tours I'd dreamed of, I threw myself into plays–I used my organizational skills to help found two off-off-Broadway theater companies in a row. I was on the management team of the second one and learned a lot about getting people to attend shows "butts in the seats." It was the bane of all small theaters. There were often more people on the stage than in the house! I grew to love writing press releases and making connections with strangers at networking events. Meanwhile, I was getting serious with the boyfriend—we had moved in together and because my ultra-Catholic parents were deeply unhappy that their only daughter was "living in sin," we were contemplating marriage to appease them. But he and I had a scheduling issue. He had gotten a day-job to make more money and his hours were 9-5 and once my theatrical career took off, mine were 9-11pm and weekends. So, I started looking for something else to do.

To pay my half of the rent, like many actors in NYC, I had been working as a temporary employee. In the beginning, I cycled through all the financial firms in New York: Bear Stearns, UBS, Lehman, even BlackRock. I worked a few law firms too—mostly what I got out of those were MeToo moments. My employers found me quick to learn and were constantly offering me full-time employment, which I airily declined, telling everyone I was an actress. They loved it. Many of them even came to my shows. But rent still had to pay, and I soon landed a gig that would last nearly five years: although I officially was a temp agency employee, I got to work at a Japanese bank on the executive floor as the assistant to the General Manager of North America. This meant I had an enormous and gloriously empty desk in a lush but tomblike corner of an elegant skyscraper with high ceilings and enormous flower arrangements and deep carpets to muffle footsteps. Apart from typing the occasional thank you note in English and booking his golf tee times, I had absolutely nothing to do except to serve tea and look pretty. Serving tea was a headache and required many consultations with the Japanese office manager who would peek in on the video cameras and let me know which gentleman to serve first, but the rest of the time on that floor was my own. The only caveat? I had to look busy.

I could not read the newspaper or a book. I had to sit up and be alert unless I was working on my computer. So, I began writing a book.

Why not? It made me look busy, and I gave a chapter at a time to my friend who was the receptionist on our floor. They also required her to look busy and had even less official work than I did. She would edit the chapter and then return it to me. I would rewrite it or give her the next chapter, depending on her notes.

Meanwhile, I got married. My husband went through his own career changes and I followed him through them. I worked so he could be a writer–he discovered that given infinite time; he wrote less and cooked more, so he left the artistic path in favor of a more steady income: first a stockbroker, then a computer instructor, a programmer, then project manager, and a few more iterations of a corporate career. I remained a temp, pursuing acting in my free time and on weekends, and auditioning during my lunch hours. I had written to chapter thirteen of my novel but did not yet consider myself a writer.

Then came the day when another secretary accused me of stealing her paper clips. She was red in the face, shaking the empty dish from across the room. There was a closet full of office supplies not three steps from her desk without even a list of inventory. You just went in and took what you needed. Still, she screamed at me and I defended myself and denied the theft, and at the end of our three-minute argument, I knew my time at the bank was over. The last thing I wanted to be was a woman who argued over paper clips.

So, I settled on getting a graduate degree. I had always loved school: they give you requirements, and if you meet them you are a celebrated success. The cleanliness of that system was very comforting to me. I had already changed identities so many times I hardly knew myself, much less my purpose in life. It would be good to once again have clear steps to follow.

I studied creative writing, since I was already writing a novel. I submitted the pages I had written to three schools: NYU (because people in theater had mentioned this was a good school), Bennington (because they had a brand-new low-residency program, the first in the country), and Columbia (because I had gotten married in the campus chapel a few years before, and thought the quad was properly academic).

Yes–I was that naïve. I did not know these schools were not equal. Sometimes being entirely ignorant can be a blessing.

NYU and Bennington rejected me within days, each with a note that although my writing was very good, since I had never taken a writing workshop, they didn't think I had the fortitude for their system of teaching. Columbia sent an elegant letter on heavy bond paper, congratulating me on acceptance to the top writing school in New York City, second this year only to Iowa in the entire country. My hand shook when I tried to put the letter back into its embossed envelope.

The universe had made me a writer.

I studied under incredible teachers; Michael Cunningham was the best of them. He sat at the head of a table full of hungry young things and wondered aloud if it was stupid to write a novel comparing his mother to Virginia Woolf. He pushed us to experiment. To thrive. To surprise ourselves. I picked up similar gems from Joyce Johnson, Helen Schulman, Stephen Koch, Lucie-Brock Broido, Richard Howard. I worked hard and produced many pages. I completed a manuscript of a novel in my five years at school, published another two poems, won a Columbia Writing Fellowship, and was well on my way to success.

My father died two weeks before the graduation ceremony.

My father was the reason I loved words. He learned English as a second language, only arriving in the country at nine, but by the time I was of age, he had mastered it. We played relentless Scrabble whenever I was home from college, and my first published story was about a young woman coming home to tell her father she wanted to donate a kidney to him—in the story they had the discussion over a Scrabble game. They published it in the

Bellevue Literary Review, and they invited me to do a public reading of the story alongside Phillip Lopate in Bellevue's beautiful and historic rotunda.

My father solved the NY Times crossword puzzle in pen before bed each night, and I never knew whether the few squares he left unfinished were because he'd gotten stuck, or because he wanted me to feel the satisfaction of completion. He was a research chemist in inorganic chemistry, and I grew up saying that tongue twister to all my new acquaintances and sounding out to him the lists of chemical preservatives in my breakfast cereal, grape jelly, and favorite snacks. My mother was the reader–always lost in a library book–but my father was the wordsmith.

And before my writing career had even begun, my father was gone. My parents had only come to New York City twice: nine years earlier for my wedding and four years after that, the summer before I started graduate school. I felt the loss of him never seeing the Financial District loft that my husband and I had finally saved up to buy. Never seeing the children, we might or might not have.

It made me wonder if I had made a mistake.

But I had a graduation to get through, and then an apartment to decorate, a mother and three brothers to comfort, and I had no time to worry about starting a family.

Three months later, on a clear, lustrous morning in early September, two jetliners flew into the office buildings across the street from our new apartment. The vibrant neighborhood we had fallen in love with over the summer vanished under debris. The Borders bookstore a block away closed. The nightly movies, jazz concerts, and comedy shows on the plaza were over. The sculpture on the water we had watched Canadian dancers gracefully build every sunset for a week, forgotten. Everything we had known gone down to the subway stations we relied upon. We could no longer trust that waking up in the morning could be a peaceful event. Our friends had lost friends, so these endless and multiple fears and traumas seemed petty. We downplayed our minor disappointments and smaller losses and kept them to ourselves. Our lives were in shambles. We lived on the floor of my mother-in-law's apartment for a month and then returned to our apartment to find it covered in dust, and without internet or phone service. We had to keep the windows closed to keep out the smell of the fires. I wrote short stories set during 9-11 and abandoned the novel that had won grants and awards but that my agent had been unsuccessful in selling. I began writing another novel while around me the EPA checked for air quality and carried off our sofa and rugs. Life was increasingly proving to be short and unpredictable.

Unsurprisingly, we got pregnant.

And that baby changed everything.

HOW PEN PARENTIS BEGAN

Gild Hall, a Thompson Hotel, first Salons location 2009-2013 with authors
Arthur Phillips and Julie Klam and host M M De Voe in April 2009.

My son was born healthy and hilarious in July 2002. I never stopped writing, even came up with the idea for a creative nonfiction book: I'd had an emergency C-section and thought a voice-driven first-person memoir peppered with second-person commentary from a doctor to explain why all the "bad" things were happening would be a great way to introduce women to the freakish road that awaits you if you have to have a c-section. Now there are hundreds of books like this, both self-published and not, but memoir was new, pregnancy treated reverentially, and no one was interested in this kind of book. My second novel had also not sold. I began writing a third.

My daughter was born in 2006. I was still writing and placing a few stories a year, winning awards for my short fiction. My fourth novel, though unpublished, had been a finalist for the Bellwether Prize and had won a grant from the Arch and Bruce Brown Foundation for Gay Positive Historical Fiction. I was meeting with friends from grad school and most of them had books out by now, many which had achieved great acclaim. The successes of my classmates inspired me to keep writing, though my mother urged me to give it up for the sake of my children.

"You'll be too tired," she said. As a mother of four, she had been the very active founder and director of the first Montessori preschool in our town—I don't think I ever saw her not pregnant or nursing. So, I ignored her advice.

Instead, I wrote every day, many hours per day. I wrote another novel and had just introduced myself at parties as "a writer working on a collection of unpublished novels," when my neighbor, Loretta Shapiro, a talented visual artist, informed me of a local arts grant. She had injured her ankle and couldn't attend the information session, and she asked, as it was the last session they were offering, if I might go in her place and take notes.

Again, my life twisted into something new.

The grant was the Manhattan Community Arts Fund, and the location was the Lower Manhattan Cultural Council, which had just received an unexpected extra $250,000 to give away to restore arts programs to the devastated neighborhood around the ruins of the World Trade Center, where I lived. A thrilled grants administrator announced that now was the time to come up with a brilliant new interactive project, and, to my delight, added that they particularly sought projects in literature. I walked out of the session bursting with plans, and immediately called my friend and writing colleague, Arlaina Tibensky, who was the only grant writer I knew. She and I had long been having lunches around the central topic: how the hell does a writer finish a novel if they have a baby.

We tried to win funds for a daylong symposium to bring writers who have kids together for panel discussions on how to finish a novel if you have a baby. We called it "Pens & Pacifiers." We thought we could do a daylong event with panels like: Creative energy and how to maintain it when breastfeeding. Office space and where to find it amid the diaper genies and bouncy chairs. How to start a college fund on an author's nebulous income. Where to find a writing group that won't mind an occasional story about mac & cheese and how to clean it off sofas. How to find a last-minute sitter and when do you need one. And how to get over the guilt of "stealing" time from the baby to write.

Remember, this was 2008. No one was talking about writing parents and their unique needs. No author was even mentioning their kids in writing bios! Even though CEOs were putting them in their personal notes when applying for jobs, writer-parents had to be like Ernest Hemingway. Artistic genius could only result from being neglectful of your children and other irresponsible behavior.

I didn't buy this.

We didn't win the grant for the "Pens & Pacifiers" symposium. They told us it was too educational. What they wanted to fund was something that brought art to people directly.

"Like a reading series?" I asked during the post-mortem with the funding agency. "A reading series featuring only the works of writers who are parents?"

"We could probably fund that," the voice on the phone mused, "Try for it next year."

The first Pen Parentis After Work Reading Series event, funded by New York City's Department of Cultural Affairs administered by the LMCC, held on the second Tuesday of January 2009. The writers were Leigh Newman and Jennifer Epstein, both young moms. On that day, Newman—now a co-founder of a publishing company and books editor on Oprah's website—premiered a memoir she was working on. She read from it in manuscript form, off typing paper that shook and rattled as she nervously asked us to be kind. That memoir, Still Points North, became a best-seller and ended up as a finalist for the National Book Critics Circle's John Leonard First Book Prize. The book Epstein premiered, The Painter from Shanghai, was a Barnes and Nobles Discover Great New Writers selection and Top 10 Debut for 2008, and a Book-of-the-Month Club First Fiction Award Nominee. Published in 16 countries, it was an international bestseller.

These were writer-parents.

Early Pen Parentis Reading Series photo - Cara Hoffman smiles as Rebecca Barry
signs a book for a fan at Todd English's The Libertine in March 2009

In 2010, because of an overwhelming response from the readers and audience that the series showed something necessary, I considered turning Pen Parentis into an organization or business venture. I knew it was vital to value the effort that new parents put into their writing, so started a Fellowship; the Pen Parentis Writing Fellowship for New Parents, giving a single writer with a child under ten a $1,000 prize and a reading in New York. I was ready to fund the prize myself if it didn't break even through reading fees.

I sent submission guidelines all over the country to various MFA programs and responses poured in. Nearly every entry had a handwritten note on the cover page thanking Pen Parentis for acknowledging the effort that parents made to remain on top of their creative careers. It was edifying. I had made the judging blind–so that talent would rise to the top. We had around seventy entries. Arlaina agreed to help me read through them and together we chose a winner—a story that made us sit up and listen, that had a voice that screamed to be heard and was irreverent and funny but also kind and caring. And in fact, from our very first fellow, Abby Sher, Pen Parentis Fellows has embodied an extraordinary level of not only talent but also dedication to writing. These are all parents of very young children. Many of the applications arrived in the mail with a note enclosed thanking us for appreciating the hard work they were putting in, or better still, saying that they had been about to give up writing for good when this award made them think twice about their decision.

Our mailing list reached to the thousands.

I had wild dreams then, of turning Pen Parentis into a profitable business. I started attending free classes given by the Small Business Administration. I found mentors and online webinars on fundraising and business structures. I filed for a DBA. I invited Arlaina to join me in the venture. She Writes founded in 2009 was raking in millions, just because people happened to be both women and writers. I thought for sure, if we also provided resources to keep people on creative track, Pen Parentis could do the same. I just needed a partner, and I was ready to take on the universe! But my friend was pregnant with her second child and was circling the wagons around her growing family. She wanted to buy a house and had no desire to become a business partner in a risky venture. She gave me her blessing to do what I would with the idea but wanted no part beyond curating the salons. It was a tear-streaked lunch, but it didn't quench the fire I had to create something larger from this amazing idea. Her response did one thing: I stopped heading down the risky for-profit route and concentrated on applying for grants. I got a fiscal sponsor so that people could donate. I attended nonprofit webinars and Meetups.

And very soon thereafter, Pen Parentis, Ltd, was born.

In 2013, a young law associate from the neighborhood suggested that we officially incorporate as a nonprofit. Her law firm, Milbank Tweed Hadley & McCoy was one of the top firms in New York City, and she felt that our programs spoke for themselves. We had corporate sponsorship from the Thompson chain of hotels who provided space and marketing through their luxurious Gild Hall Hotel and Todd English's restaurant in the Financial District where we held our events—now rechristened Pen Parentis Literary

Salons. I had already won many years of grants from New York City and New York State arts councils. Busy with house hunting and in the throes of publishing a young adult novel, Arlaina declined to be on the initial board, but two other friends jumped in: Emily Speer became our treasurer and Michael Del Castillo volunteered to be secretary. With their help and the help of the law firm, we attained 501c3 status easily and quickly, and I embarked on the career of executive director of a nonprofit.

I had no experience. No background. No idea what I was doing or where I was taking everyone. All I had was the firm knowledge that parents were no different from non-parents except that they had fewer resources to work with: less time, less money, and less energy. Each and every literary salon told me the same thing: if you want to write, you can write. You just have to figure out your resources.

So that became the goal of Pen Parentis: to provide resources to writers to keep them on creative track after they start a family.

And here we are—we had a crazy few glitches: the few times that a co-host would suddenly quit or travel and I had to scramble to find a replacement, the time Hurricane Sandy blew out our amps, the sudden blizzard that canceled three internationally bestselling writers, and the crazy day, two weeks before our September 11, 2011 Salon, when the Gild Hall Hotel forgot to let us know that they'd evicted their Todd English restaurant and taken in a new restaurant which had gutted the library where we were scheduled to have a salon!

That day, I walked down the street to the Andaz Wall Street (a Hyatt boutique hotel) which had been courting us for months and offered them our next event. A glorious five-year partnership was born. During those years, the Andaz hotel not only hosted the salons for free but also provided wine and an array of nibbles for our audiences. Sometimes I arrived to set up only to discover the room arranged for a morning event in an entirely new style, or that our room was occupied by a paying client and we had been relocated to a different space–but these were easy accommodations for someone trained in Improv theater.

What a run! Ten years of salons with breaks only in the summer months. And even then, I'm a little crazy, so in the summers we did impromptu things like partner up with Mutha Magazine for a House of Lit party where we took over an incredible historical three-story house on Governor's Island off Manhattan and filled it with kid-friendly activities for no other reason than to have spread the love of storytelling to the next generation. Summer special events have also included a Pirates & Mermaids books party for kids on a lighthouse tender, a low-cost class featuring actors teaching writers how best to choose and perform a public reading, some rooftop parent-writer Meetups... And then Covid-19 hit and every one of our programs went immediately online. What a scramble that was—but how lovely that our Meetups can now welcome writers from Arizona, Ohio, and Boston! I am eager to see what the next ten years bring. And in the meantime, Pen Parentis is going strong.

I am so proud whenever a new writer sends me a note from Idaho or Missouri and tells me they came across Pen Parentis on Facebook, Twitter or Instagram, and were inspired to keep writing just because of our existence. It makes me want to spread the inspiration everywhere. I hope that with this book, I might share some things our authors have taught us all over the years about resilience, perseverance, and above all, dedication to their writing careers.

Good luck with your parenting and writing,

-M. M. De Voe

Founder, Pen Parentis, Ltd

EVERY ACTIVIST NEEDS A MANIFESTO

How can any one person be an expert on being a writer-parent?

There isn't even an appropriate term for the situation we find ourselves in: parent-writer, writer-parent, mom-writer, dad-writer? None of these encompass the cognitive dissonance that ordinary people feel when you tell them you are both a writer and a parent. The assumptions are quick: "oh, you write children's books?" or "you blog about your kids?" "You're a stay at-home parent with a hobby?"

No.

I'm a professional literary artist and I happen to have children.

I hold an MFA from Columbia University in Creative Writing. I have been a Columbia University Writing Fellow, a Summer Literary Seminars Writing Fellow (the fellowship took me to St. Petersburg in Russia for two weeks while my daughter was 18 months old). I have just returned from the inaugural Writers Forum in Lithuania where I was one of 45 writers from 18 countries representing the Lithuanian Diaspora Writing Community. I have won more than 20 literary awards, and cash prizes for everything from an unpublished novel to a Twitter poem about NYC. I have published short pieces in every genre from science fiction, horror and urban fantasy to literary flash. I have taught workshops, worked on the editorial board of a literary journal and doctored books for published writers—the only thing I have yet to do in my writing career is pen a best seller, but I know a dozen writers who are parents who have not only done that but also won top literary awards. Jennifer Egan won the Pulitzer Prize and had to compare it to a soccer tournament to get her young sons to comprehend the enormity of the win. Victor LaValle posts about his two kids on social media between mentions of his various literary and cross-genre awards and his symbolic possession of the Key to Queens. Kelly Link has a lovely daughter and a MacArthur Fellowship (commonly known as a Genius Award). At Pen Parentis we have featured the critically acclaimed writing of over 300 writers who are also parents.

We are writers.

The fact that we have children has no effect on our talent.

Parenthood is not a career. You don't get paid for it. There is no university-level course to teach you to do it. There are not even any parenting experts that are not self-proclaimed. There are no parenting awards. There is no guarantee that what works in one instance will ever work again, even in similar circumstances, even in the same family unit.

> *Parenthood is not a profession.*
> *It is a life-event.*
> *A life-changing event that is momentous and amazing and irreversible.*
> *Parenthood is a responsibility you bear.*
> *It is not a career.*

The problem with trying to address the unique difficulties of being a writer-parent, is that career and parenthood are two distinct things that our society constantly tries to conflate. They are actually quite disparate—as our language shows us when we attempt to create a phrase that means both. Career and family should NEVER be considered substitutes for each other. You don't have a child (or take a lover!) to replace your career, and your career does not fill "the place where a child should be." To think along those lines is appalling and disrespectful of both career and family.

Let me repeat this yet again because this is at the heart of Pen Parentis and everything we believe: Career and family are distinct entities in life and should be considered and addressed independently of each other. One is something you do, the other is a responsibility you have.

My friends: It is possible to have both a successful career and a thriving family.

Really.

BECOMING A PARENT IS A LIFE EVENT

My bachelor uncle once wrote this cynical version of parenthood.

"The biological world is a simple place: if an embryo is viable, it is generally born. If nothing happens to the child, it reaches puberty. The young human continues to age, barring accidents and disease, it lives for as long as the life span allows and then it dies. Some amount of these humans procreate along the way. This ensures that other humans are born. The biological goal of humanity is to create a circumstance whereby offspring live long enough to procreate themselves. That's it. That's parenthood. It's a biological system to ensure that humanity continues to exist on the planet."

It's a life event. You are a parent, even if you flee your responsibilities. You remain a parent, even if you don't know that you fathered a child. You are a mother, even if you left your infant on your great aunt Mary's doorstep and now live in Antarctica. Parenthood is not something you DO; it is something you ARE.

But oh, the verb form of that word.

While the Oxford English Dictionary began listing parenthood as a noun in 1918, the first use of the word "parent" as a verb only occurred in 1959. Before that there was the intriguing 1930s word "parent craft" (used to discuss those strange people, who were hyper-involved in raising their own children rather than hiring nannies and governesses to do the work).

"Parenting" as a concept is new. Yet it is a popular topic, and this has created a plethora of contradicting experts happy to advise you for a fee—not to mention the self-proclaimed experts who will happily advise you, a total stranger, for free as they walk down the street and catch a glimpse of you with your child.

The point is, that the verb form of "parent" is a very recent creation.

And yet, the publishing industry has discovered an enormous market for books about this verb—it is a vast black hole of information. According to science, parenthood is a medical subject—parenting "experts" have traditionally been psychologists and sociologists divided by method into groups of thought (Dr. Benjamin Spock, B. F. Skinner, John B. Watson, Jean Piaget, Alfie Kohn, the list is endless, and more often than not, also childless and male).

Have a look at Amazon's top selling parenting books: The #1 bestseller in the category of parenting on October 22, 2019, was a coloring book for girls. #2 was an actress' memoir and #3 was Rich Dad, Poor Dad. You have to scroll down to #13 to find the first book by a PhD, who not only claims to be an expert, but seems to release a new book every year to prove it (he has another one coming out in 2020). Let us assume, then, that sales = expertise. Other than this author, the most notably followed recent book is "The Science of Parenthood," published in 2006, which draws on "ten years of research"—not even a child's full life span—and was originally self-published by a psychologist who as far as I can tell, has no kids of her own. She claims "over twenty" books to her name, but upon some research, most of them have names like "A Pea Called Mildred"— picture books about some aspect of mental wellness for children.

I haven't read these books, this isn't a criticism of parenting books, I'm just pointing out that with the proper doctorate, almost any good nonfiction research-based writer can be an expert in parenthood because it's not really a field. It's a book-selling category that showed up around the 1960s.

However: people have been having babies since the dawn of time. And they have (mostly) been trying to keep those babies alive. And also, for the most part, trying to keep them happy. (Imagine how many stone caves echo—I am sure that Neanderthal mamas and papas were just as interested in having baby-BamBam stop crying as today's loft-dwelling Brooklyn parent.) Having a child puts you in an enormous group of humanity.

It is estimated that 89.615% of the humans on the planet will ultimately procreate (according to data statistician Anshul Rajan). Parenting is something every one of these humans will also do. Even people who have their children taken away because of neglect or abuse are parents. Negligent parents, granted, but still parents. Birth mothers? Sperm donors? All parents—as evidenced by the many children from loving adoptive homes who still want to meet their biological parents (out of sheer curiosity, if nothing more). We all have genuine relationships to our parents, whether they are alive, whether we love them or hate them, and this relationship form us. Our parents form us. Obviously when we become parents, we will, to some extent, form our own kids. And naturally, we want to do what's best. What's right. Incredible that there is an activity that 90% of us take on with no clue of the right way to do it.

But wait—is there a right way?

There are multiple wrong ways!

But maybe parenting is like swimming—where if you make it back into the boat without drowning or getting caught in the boat's propellers, it really doesn't matter whether you did a perfect butterfly stroke or coughed up some water. Your lungs burn. Your eyes sting. You feel grateful to have survived the trip, and on the boat goes.

Perhaps good parenting is merely working your way through a series of crises with whatever combination of inner judgement, instinct, outside advice and example, help and luck available to you.

Seems to me that if there were a "right way" or even a "better way" to parent—one that would guarantee results with 100% of the children 100% of the time, humanity would have figured that out by now. There would be a unified approach to parenting. Instead, over 60,000 books are for sale on parenting. That's sixty thousand opinions powerful enough that someone bothered to write a book about it—not to mention the endless blogs, essays, and articles on the topic.

No wonder new parents are overwhelmed.
Parenting is not a science. It is a topic of conversation.

A STORY FROM THE VERY FIRST SALON

Jennifer Cody Epstein

This is an excerpt from the transcript of our first event, on January 9, 2009, at what we then called The Pen Parentis After Work Reading Series.

In a then brand-new Todd English restaurant called The Libertine on the second floor of a swanky Thompson Hotel, the Gild Hall on Gold Street in the Financial District, **Jennifer Cody Epstein** had these words to say to our very first audience:

"As two my former classmates will testify, I was about halfway through Columbia when I got [laughter] knocked up. I remember having a woman say to me in one of my classes I was crazy for having a baby because I would never be a writer now. And I remember being just so stricken by this because all I wanted to *do* was to be a writer. I have to say—she was wrong.

I had the postpartum breakdown—*what am I going to do with my life? I'm not sleeping? I look like hell and I can't focus enough to brush my teeth,* but then, you know I kind of got out of it with some help from a very fed-up husband. And I just started writing, and it was an enforced deadline: I had until the baby woke up every day, and I found when I had that kind of pressure, I was so much more productive.

I wrote the first half of *Painter from Shanghai* when my daughter was between three months and a year and a half. I think it just kind of forced me to grow up and take my writing more seriously."

Jennifer Cody Epstein's novel *The Painter from Shanghai* became an international bestseller.

She is also author of a national bestseller, *Wunderland*, which was long listed for the Joyce Carol Oates/Simpson Project literary award. Her second novel, *The Gods of Heavenly Punishment*, won the 2014 Asian Pacific Association of Librarians Honor award for outstanding fiction. She has written for *The Wall Street Journal*, *The Asian Wall Street Journal*, *The Nation* (Thailand), *Self* and *Mademoiselle* magazines, and the NBC and HBO networks, while working in Kyoto, Tokyo, Hong Kong and Bangkok, and Washington D.C. and New York. She has taught at Columbia University in New York and Doshisha University in Kyoto, and holds an MFA from Columbia, a Masters of International Relations from the Johns Hopkins School of Advanced International Studies, and a BA in Asian Studies/English from Amherst College. At the writing of this book, she is living in Brooklyn with husband, filmmaker Michael Epstein, and two daughters.

These are the kinds of stories that the writers who read at Pen Parentis tell. Struggle, yes. But also, the ultimate victory.

ARTISTS AS PARENTS

Parenthood is a life event.

It is a choice for many, a surprise for a few. It has repercussions. It is forever. It changes you—like puberty, like marriage, like the death of a parent, like all other life events. There is joy and there is fear. There is sorrow. It is so much bigger than what social media would like you to believe.

Ah. There's the rub.

It's huge, and who can you trust? Those "experts" on the bookshelves? Pick a trend. Maybe you want to educate yourself? You can get a degree in Parent-Educating, but you can't get a degree in Parenting itself. Think about that.

Parenting is a thing you learn by doing—and ironically? There are no right answers, only wrong answers that you hope never to do again.

As sung about in that wonderful long-running musical, *The Fantasticks*, if you plant a radish, you'll get a radish...but there is no guarantee with a child that anything a parent does will have the desired result.

Is this getting depressing? It shouldn't be. Remember your own childhood? You survived it. Sure, it could have been better, but then again, maybe not. Improve what you can. Embrace the uncertainty and keep on doing your personal best.

But this isn't a parenting book, it's a book about writing.

In 2018, the prolific and highly acclaimed writer, Michael Chabon, wrote an article for GQ *magazine*, which begins with an anecdote from the night of his wedding to Ayelet Waldman. A famous unnamed writer advises him against having children. Each child, this famous writer says, is a novel never published. Michael Chabon married anyway, and the literary couple went on to have four children. His wife has published seven novels, and he has published fourteen.

He also won the Pulitzer Prize.

So has Jennifer Egan. And Viet Than Nguyen. And Paul Harding. And Anthony Doerr. (All are recent Pulitzer Prize-winning fiction writers who mention their kids upfront in their bios.)

But here's the kicker. GQ blurbed Chabon's article (here is a link if you would like to read the entire article: **https://www.gq.com/story/michael-chabon-are-kids-the-enemy-of-writing**) with this lede: "Here, Chabon (father of four) *considers what was lost* when he defiantly ignored that advice."

What was *lost*?

Yes, this is clickbait just trying to get the reader to go to the article, but clickbait reinforces stereotypes. Clickbait preys on your very natural fears—four foods you should never eat if you want to be productive, ten shows to watch to avoid dying in your sleep, six wines that reduce belly fat — these establish a fear in the reader (getting fired, dying, weight gain) and then purport to solve them in some easy way. The GQ sub-header for Michael Chabon's article solidifies a stereotype that already exists in people's minds (that writing, and parenting are incompatible). But instead of playing with that fear (you CAN be a writer and a parent! Michael Chabon crushes the negative stereotype of writer-parent) it suggests that all parents automatically fall short as writers, that Michael Chabon and Ayelet Waldman—and their fourteen plus seven novels and a Pulitzer Prize are inherently a writing failure—because if only they had chosen not to have kids, it would have been more.

Because of the stereotype of artist-as-parent, instead of the article celebrating Chabon's accomplishments, it suggests that parenthood held him back—even though the article (and his life!) states the opposite.

This is what we fight against at Pen Parentis.

No one would ever fault a childless author for publishing "only" seven novels. In fact, many legendary writers have only written one novel: Emily Bronte, Harper Lee, Ralph Ellison...all had only one book. And zero children.

Parenthood does not affect talent. Becoming a parent changes, you, yes. In particular, it takes away many of the resources that you might otherwise have given to your writing career. Most notably parenthood takes time, money, and energy. Becoming a parent affects your life like any other major life event. It is uncanny that articles are written about how parenthood can steal from your writing career, but not how, for example, caring for your aging parents will do the same thing. No one writes exposés about how great sex with a scintillating partner is distracting from your writing career. So why is society hellbent on criticizing artists for having kids?

We may never have an answer to that question. But what we *can* do is to help emerging writers see that it is only propaganda. Writers with kids do great things all the time. It requires dedication, commitment, and having a strong will. It requires dealing with a lot of guilt. But it can be done.

And we think that's a *good* thing.

Let's address the resources you'll need to replenish, one by one.

Ready? Let's go.

PART 2

Writing with An Infant

WRITING WITH AN INFANT

Time

Starting a family definitely leaves the new parent with less time. Even before Baby arrives, there is furniture to assemble and decisions to make on nursery colors and recently, what pronouns to use. Naming a child is as hard in reality as it is to name a main character in a new story—only this little character will grow up to demand your reasons. Hey, no one said parenthood was easy: there's plenty of downside to the investments you'll make. However, there are vast upsides too: characters in books will not hug you with pride when you win your Nobel Prize and they also won't cry at your funeral.

Just saying.

Let's accept that babies take time. Lots of time. First, they steal your sleep in a manner that the Geneva Conventions consider torture. Then they are adorable to look at while *they* sleep, so even if you get them down at a reasonable hour, expect to lose the next ten minutes in dizzy gaping at the miracle that the gorgeous living creature you can't stop looking at is a biological creature that you yourself have created—most times by doing nothing more than enjoying yourself with the person you most love in the world. You made a new human! That's pretty distracting. Maybe forever. But it's also a really cool thing. Most of the positive aspects of having a kid are cool things. Kid-laughter, kid cuteness, kid wide-eyed wonder...

Okay – baby bonuses aside, let's talk about how you will write when you have to allocate your time resource almost entirely to your helpless and adorable offspring: You'll figure this one out as it goes.

I'm not kidding. There's no method that works for everyone. You'll figure it out as it goes. You'll try a few things, and some will work, and some won't.

Hey, don't toss this book aside. This isn't a parenting guide. It is a *writing* guide. The parenting part is unique to your kid and your family unit, whatever that is. Some babies are easy and have regular naptimes and sleep during those nap times and again at night. Some babies feed on schedule. Some are not at all colicky and wake to enjoy the world. If you have one of these babies, you are always going to write when the baby is sleeping. Yeah, sure, they tell you to sleep when the baby is sleeping. You can do that too. To be perfectly honest, the first three months of the baby's life is a swirl of "Holy cats, how in the ninth circle of hell am I ever going to manage this. I made a baby. It's a real human life! I did this. This baby exists because of me. Wow. How am I ever going to manage?"

And that's normal.

Your thoughts will spiral so extremely out of control, you may cry over you not knowing how you're going to pay for college or how you will react if your baby brings home a lover you dislike. I'm not kidding, you'll be living in future fears and past recriminations, and the present moment will always be terrifying or heartbreakingly beautiful, or so frustrating you won't believe you can go on. You will doubt yourself and you will beam with pride. You will stare at tiny fingernails like they are a wonder of the world and you will care wildly about things you can't believe you are even thinking about like dust, ibuprofen, tiny socks, and ambient sound.

And that's fine.

Learn new skills.

Love your baby.

Find your schedule.

Figure it out.

You can do this, because you are the parent. People have been dealing with these same problems since the first baby was born. How does one support a family and still protect and comfort their children? One does what is important. What is important? A lot of that is subjective. Get off the crazy-wheel of social media, stop reading articles and blogs by "expert" parents—when they had their first baby, they didn't know any better than you did. Get in touch with your own inner self—what is important to *you*? Those are the values to instill in your child, and the best way to do that is by example. Now you can go back to the blogs and the social media posts if you want to. Keep a sense of humor. Use what works. Throw away everything else.

Is writing a priority? It was for me. I found time...no; I *made* time for my writing. Recognize up front that "writing" won't look the same as it did before you had a baby—but then neither will showering, eating dinner, or sleeping. These things, if they were ever important to you, will become more precious and you will treasure any time you find to do any of them.

I promise.

Instead of rules, let's talk possibilities:

What can writing look like after a baby?

In the first three months or even more, if you don't write a single word, it truly doesn't matter. People take writing breaks all the time and for much stupider reasons than the care of a helpless, dependent human being. People stop writing for three months because they go on a cruise to Antarctica, get a high-powered job, get in an ugly fight with their boyfriend, go broke and have to figure out where to live, get arrested, get bed bugs in their house, decide they have to go back to school, hit a wall and just can't deal. People take breaks. This does not mean that your writing career is shot.

You might. You might not. It will depend a lot on your baby, and who you are as a parent. No judgement, and there should not be any. People are different. Babies are different. You will do what you can. You'll do what feels right. Let that happen and don't fret there is no right way to do this.

Here are a bunch of things you can do for your writing without opening up the document on your laptop.

You can think about plot. You can come up with crazy character names. You can talk about the situations you're going to put your characters in. You can take long walks (even pushing a stroller!) and think about plot twists. If you are a poet, you might think about forms, about words, you might analyze how different the world looks, you might make lists. You can jot down notes! You can read! Upon becoming a parent, you will be connected to history and the universe in a way you can't imagine before you have a child. There's a bit of an "aha" moment after you hold your baby for the first time—where you suddenly realize that your own parents also didn't have a clue, that no one in history has ever had a clue, and that the bossy woman who tells you she had ten kids who is giving you parenting advice from across a crowded airplane might give you a sage pearl of wisdom or a piece of garbage, no one knows. The advice might even work on your first child, but not at all on your second! Each child is different. You are also unique as a parent. All of this is normal and okay.

So: in these first three months, take the pressure off. Write when you feel like it, read if you have the energy, do what feels right. Just live your life. Think of it as maternity or paternity leave. Bond with the baby and enjoy how tiny they are. Stare at them. Laugh with them. Enjoy them.

(If you're crazy like me, you might read those piled-up New Yorker short stories aloud to your baby, just so you have time to read them yourself. You might also write some freaky poetry. Sleep-deprived brains are weird.)

After the first three months, the baby is more alert, more responsive. Many parents feel more guilt about leaving them alone for even short periods of time. This is normal and you will work your way through this. At six months, your baby will move - you will long for the days when you could put them down and they would stay. The toys get bigger and louder. The demands are followed by louder insistence. Things are changing, but this is still the easy part of parenting (even though it can feel overwhelmingly impossible) - so hang in there and do your best.

When can you write? Anytime you can make the time. Notice I didn't say "find" - I said "make" - this is the hardest time to sit down and write unless your baby is a fantastic sleeper, or you have the world's best support system and no capacity for guilt. I would say at age 6 months is when most writers who give up on their writing careers usually throw in the towel. The guilt is too heavy, the fear of failure too great. You have this infant who enjoys your company, and then you have this novel manuscript that may or may never be finished. The temptation to give up and "put it off until they start school" will be overwhelming.

It's a choice. If you take that path, you will be seven years or more behind on your writing career. That doesn't mean you'll never have a novel. Many brilliant novels have been written by parents who took a break to raise their kids. It is a path and you have to own your own path. If you give it up, don't criticize other parents who don't feel whole unless they do write a paragraph or two every few days. Don't be jealous of the mom who wins an international short fiction award and meets the Queen of Spain, while her two kids are under seven. (Looking at you, Emily Raboteau!) Truly though - at our salons we have seen parents who gave up their writing for the entire time they were raising kids. It is the same as taking a break from being a lawyer or taking a break from being an acrobat. You will either come back with a vengeance, or you won't ever come back. But there is never a guarantee in the arts that you will "make it" in the first place, even if you methodically work hard, diligently attend all the 'right' schools, and meet all the powerful people. No guarantee.

So, follow your heart. Be true to yourself and your needs. If what you need is to stop writing novels and write poetry instead, do that. If you need to put it all down and be a daddy, do that. If you win a writing fellowship to research anacondas in the rainforest, do it! Take your kid along! What a wonderful education. What an interesting kid you will have when they grow up.

You will make your own rules and guidelines about how and when and where you make time to write.

Write that sentence on a post-it and stick it to your laptop.

Perhaps you will write one hour every day after baby goes down for the night. Perhaps you are lucky, and when you wake one hour before the rest of the house, your baby doesn't psychically know it and wake to join you (many babies do and this is so frustrating to the writing parents who try to sneak in an hour of writing time before baby is up!). Maybe you stay up one hour later than you'd like and then nap with the baby mid-morning. Maybe you will just use an app or carry a piece of paper to jot down ideas so that on a Saturday morning, your spouse, significant other, best friend, or paid babysitter can take your baby for a walk leaving you to scramble to make a comprehensible flash piece out of the idea you jotted on the back of a dry cleaning slip. And maybe you're the parent of a special-needs baby and you won't have one second to yourself and one day you will sit down after two months of no writing and you will write a short poem which is messy and has no point and that will be all the writing you manage in the first year of your kid's life. It's fine. There are no right answers. There is only experimentation and willpower at this stage. Every baby is different. Every writer is different.

I say again: figure it out.

You're a smart cookie, and you *can* do this.

At Pen Parentis, we offer writer-parent Meetups that encourage writers to set personal goals, and the group accountability helps new parents meet those goals. Several of our meet-up regulars have infants. Their schedules change all the time, usually just at the moment that you've finally settled into a new routine. We find that setting a weeklong goal is best, because when you are a parent there are always things that come up on a day-by-day basis, but if you have a weeklong goal and someone holding you accountable at the end of the week, the goals are more likely to be accomplished, even if they have to be crammed into the last day!

Some ideas for week-long goals are:

- *Write 250 words*
- *Edit a final draft of a short story and send it out*
- *Write a new chapter*
- *Jot down ideas for a month of blog posts*
- *Find ten appropriate places to send your latest essay and then send it out*
- *Read two chapters of a how-to-publish book*
- *Query five agents*
- *Write 15 minutes every day*
- *Make a list of 10 descriptions of places or people or events, or even common items*
- *Write a character map for your novel*
- *Research 30 minutes for your historical fiction*
- *Outline the first third of a new novel*

The most effective goals, we have found at the Meetups, are the ones with specificity. Strive for a particular word count or number of pages. (You can always go over—but a numerical goal is a great way to feel a sense of accomplishment.) Don't just "write every day", instead write X-X-number of minutes every day. Create your own accountability—but better still, partner up with another writer or two, especially if they are also parents, and hold each other accountable. You need to know if you exceeded your goal. "I'm going to look at that short story," means that if you work on it for two minutes or ten hours, you feel the same. If you say, "I'm going to work on the story for ten minutes" and then you work for two hours, imagine how much better you will feel!

PRO-TIP: If your goal is an "every day goal"—as in you want to do something every day—make a visible calendar where you make a mark each day that you achieved your goal and as Jerry Seinfeld said about writing a new joke every day, "don't break the chain." Incidentally? Jerry Seinfeld is a dad.

Visual cues help. Rewards help. Use every trick in your arsenal. There are countless apps to help you achieve this if you are an app-addict (some that our members have recommended are: but a piece of paper with penciled check marks is just as strong as a visual cue.

Remember: there is no "right" way to do this – there is only doing what you can or having nothing done.

A STORY FROM THE SALONS

Tim Fitts

Tim Fitts lives and works in Philadelphia, where he is a professor of creative writing at the Curtis Institute of Music. He is the author of two short story collections and *The Soju Club*, a novel that was published in South Korea. He has published over thirty short stories and came to New York to read at Pen Parentis in April 2019.

Here's what he said when asked about having an infant and trying to write:

"It has always surprised me when people say that children take up too much time to write. The opposite is true. Sure, it feels like there is less time, but in actuality, we learn to make use of whatever time we have. When our first daughter was born, I used to place a blanket on the table next to my laptop and write while she slept there."

Tim related how, as they aged, his daughters developed a genuine love and knowledge of narrative. He was delighted to report that his elder daughter now takes her own creative writing projects seriously. Besides having pride in his own published work, he rests easy knowing that his children will also grow up with a love of this form, a love that will serve them well in their future educations.

A STORY FROM THE SALONS

Domenica Ruta

Domenica Ruta is a fiction writer and memoirist from Massachusetts. A scholarship kid at Phillips Academy Andover and Oberlin College, she has worked as a videographer and editor, a bookstore clerk, a waitress, a bartender, an English-as-a-Foreign-Language teacher, a nanny, a nursing home caregiver, a domestic violence hotline advocate, and a housecleaner. She received her MFA from the Michener Center for Writers at the University of Texas, Austin.

Her first book, the memoir *With or Without You*, was a *New York Times* Bestseller and named by *Entertainment Weekly* as one of the top three nonfiction books of the year 2013. *The Boston Globe*, *Macleans*, NPR, *Slate*, *Elle*, *Bust*, Oprah.com and *USA Today* all loved it.

Her first novel, *Last Day*, was released in May 2019 from Spiegel & Grau/ Penguin Random House and was critically acclaimed. She co-edited the 2019 anthology *We Got This: Solo Mom Stories of Grit, Heart and Humor*. She reviews books for the New York Times, Oprah.com and the American Scholar, and works as an editor, curator, and advocate for solo moms at ESME.com.

The following comments are compiled from her appearance on May 14, 2019, at the Tenth Anniversary Pen Parentis Salon Season Grand Finale in the Oculus at Westfield World Trade Center in New York City and from a Pen Parentis interview from about a month after that Salon.

"Being a single mom is like, I don't know, do you? Do wait till the kids go to school? Or do you write with the kids running around? I mean, how do you do this?" So, for this book (holds up *The Last Day*, laughter) — I pounded out a really ugly, awful draft of this while I was pregnant. I finished a draft of it literally a week before I gave birth.

I had no idea what was coming, but I had a feeling that writing was going to be infinitely more challenging once there was a baby there. So, I just thought it'd be easier to have, you know, a rock. You haul the rock down from the mountain and then chisel it away a little at a time — later; I figured I wouldn't have the bandwidth or the energy to haul that rock.

I wanted the rock there.

So, I had my baby, and for the first six months I wrote zero words. I wrote nothing. That was scary because, you know, I had this mantra in my head, *real writers write every day, even when it's hard,* which I now think is a tool of the white patriarchy. Because no, not if they're single moms! Not if they have to support this whole family? Anyway, there are a lot of reasons not to write every day.

I just kept telling myself, I have this rock, and I will start chiseling it when I can. When my son was about a year old, he started going to daycare two days a week and I would write those two days a week.

And then when I had the money, I did daycare five days a week and wrote five days a week. I'm being perfectly honest, I've never been very good at keeping a schedule, even before I became a mother. When my son was an infant, everyone kept lecturing me about sleep training and sleep schedules and all that. I tried to do that, but my son had other plans. One day, at one of his baby check-ups, I confessed to the pediatrician, "He doesn't have a schedule, but he has a pattern." She smiled–and she is not a smiling woman ordinarily–and told me I was wise.

I would fit in all of my freelance work with him around. I couldn't write creatively with him around at all. I just couldn't concentrate. But I could do wage-earning work from home with him around, which I did to sustain us. My whole life, including my writing life works like that–there is not a schedule with concrete appointment times but there are habits and patterns I honor.

I eventually dipped into my savings account to pay for childcare, because I was not earning enough to pay my living expenses and for childcare. The financial insecurity is terrifying. I can spend several years working on a book and there is no guarantee that it will earn me a penny. That is a huge risk to take when you have kids. I pay for health insurance out of pocket as I am the perennial freelancer with no full-time employer. I considered childcare an investment and felt I was lucky to have it, and I drained my savings account and hoped that it would pay off in the end.

And it did. Thank God."

WRITING WITH AN INFANT

Energy

While you have an infant, your baby sleeps a lot.

A *lot.* There are many two-hour breaks during the day and at night. Unfortunately, human adults need their time organized in longer chunks than one or two hours at a stretch. There is a very good chance that if you finish any writing while your baby is still a baby, what you will write is very short fiction or poetry. It is hard to keep your mind on a big project when you barely can recall the day of the week. Not enough is said about baby-brain (or mommy-brain, depending on where you live) — it is incredible how lack of sleep steals your ability to function in any effective way.

According to a study by the Allen Institute of Brain Science and SRI, sleep deprivation leads to irritability and impaired memory, lack of coordination and loss of concentration. Luckily, these conditions are temporary and getting enough sleep will reverse them. Still and all, you can't guarantee yourself eight hours of sleep (or even four!) with a newborn. So okay, you'll have trouble remembering that cool synonym for penniless that starts with a d, you won't quite know what your main character said about chocolate ice cream the day before, you'll be lucky if you even care about what happens to the new delivery man you introduced in Chapter 6, much less be able to remember how to switch from one screen to another in the newest upgrade of Scrivener. It definitely isn't the optimal situation for organized and thoughtful writing.

That said, if you let yourself get out of baby-mode and just write, you often find you are at your most creative. The flow of words and free associations is heightened, as is the desire to get them on the page. There is an urgency to the writing, a need to communicate to the reader. New parents also often find they are in a dream state once the writing begins that offers real creative flow. Isn't the stereotype that writers stay up into the wee hours, loopy on alcohol and nicotine or more, just to get out of conventional thought patterns? Believe me, you won't be more sleep deprived or loopy than when you are regularly waking every three or four hours all night for a few months. Scribble down all the dream-induced, half-baked, insane creative ideas that you have—the perfect metaphors, the lovely descriptions of moments; keep a dream journal; do all the things they mentioned in the first "how to write" webinar you ever watched. But let go of the guilt of not being as productive on the page as you were before Baby. Writing is writing. For creative writers, goals have always been self-imposed. There's no finish line you have to hit. No word count that is nationally approved as "enough for the day." So, after you have your baby, don't pressure yourself to finish things, but finish things if you can. Just be.

All the various things you think and feel while you hold your infant are the things that will make your future novel a brilliant book. You are literally holding someone's entire future in your arms—but you're not alone. People have done this for centuries. Channel that power.

What you won't have much of in the infancy stage, however, is energy. Babies are draining—yes, they are adorable, and you feel like you are part of a huge machine to keep humanity on earth (you are!) but that machine will tax you heavily in this first year. The sleep deprivation and eating weird things at weird times, and (if you're a nursing mom) being the source of food—well, it's exhausting and will physically deplete you. The idea of putting a notebook by your bed or of picking up a pencil for one second will seem like too much. You'll tell yourself you'll remember things. You'll lie to yourself the same way you did as a developing teen—promising yourself that if you just get a little time for yourself, you'll do all the things that are important for your future later.

Remember those teen years? Hearken back to them now. Grab a bit of time for yourself whenever you can. If you're like me, writing feeds your soul and writing even one glorious description of a predawn nursery will remind you you haven't lost your talent. That you are still the person you were before you reproduced—that the act of reproducing didn't fade the original (it doesn't, you know! The original stays the same, no matter how often you reproduce it!)

You are an original. Be true to yourself. Find the joy in writing and leave behind the guilt. You are not stealing from your child if you leave the laundry for half an hour while you write a beautiful string of words. In fact, as one of our writers mentioned in a Salon, "Housework is something you can always do with the kids awake."

I guess my point about energy is that you won't have any. This is a resource that is not available during the infant years. Write when you can. Be thrilled with any production at all. Truly. Celebrate any words you put on the page. Once your baby sleeps through the night (and this can take a lot longer than you expect) you'll eventually get through feeling permanently jet lagged, and your creative energy will return. In the meantime, be gentle with yourself. Free yourself from guilt. Write if you can, and if you can't, just enjoy yourself and take lots of photos of the baby.

WRITING WITH AN INFANT

Money

Which brings us to the heaviest burden: money.

Unless you are a trust fund kid or married to a very generous spouse who works in an indestructible industry, money will be your nemesis for the entire time you are a parent. Babies are expensive. They just are. Diapers, baby transport (strollers, baby Bjorns, slings, etc.) And food will be your obsession for two solid years or more. Baby enrichment is an industry that rivals the bridal industry for turning a fleeting moment of panic and joy into an enormous amount of purchasable inventory. Know your budget and be strong. Money is *going* to be an issue.

Not just the requirements like diapers, but the optionals: is baby music class, baby language class, baby art class, baby nature class.... are any of these going to be the one perfect thing that will determine that your kid is a successful adult? From the outside, I would say no, but having gone through two rounds of infants, I am not sure which of us needed these classes more—the baby or the overtired, desper- ate-to-do-something new mom.

And they are not cheap, my friends. Just because it is a college freshman sitting crisscross applesauce on a ratty rug and pressing play on her iPhone over a speaker, doesn't mean that music class is less than $60/hour.

Expect to make budget decisions that stagger you in their impracticality. And what's worse? Every one of them feels like it could be a life or death decision. Generic diapers or hand-spun organic? Let me tell you that the marketing will absolutely convince you that this is a life-or-death choice.

It won't help that nothing is less secure than writing as a profession (well, okay, maybe standup comedy) .... But the point is, as a writer, particularly a creative writer, what you are doing is investing hours, weeks, months, years, into a long-term project that may or may not get sold and for no guarantee that if it sells, you will earn anything like minimum wage. So. Face that. Do whatever you need to do to keep the baby fed and still feed your IRA and your kid's college fund. It's not easy. Many writers are also teachers, some do webinars (passive income is always wonderful), some are freelance editors, and some have second careers or day jobs to earn a living. Before your first novel sells (and often long after) writers supplement their income—if for nothing more than health insurance. Accept it and embrace it and keep making time to write. We all have to stay warm through the winter, but don't burn your manuscript to do it. This has always been a problem for writers – this income thing. Adding a child changes nothing, just makes you face up in a more realistic way to how very chancy it is to aim for a literary writing career, if your primary goal in writing is to make money.

PRO TIP: If making money is *actually* your ultimate writing goal, and you are or intend to become a writer of bestselling commercial fiction, selling essays, book reviews, and short fiction in your chosen genre might be a good placeholder during these early childhood years to build your base. Submit flash fiction to anthologies, websites, and other paid markets, get cozy with editors of magazines that review your genre of commercial fiction, and be a good literary citizen—spread the word about other writers you know who are in your genre. It is not impossible to make a living if you write commercial fiction. Genres like crime fiction, horror, science fiction, mystery, and fantasy currently pay up to $.10/word for excellent individual short stories and are always looking for well-written narratives. These markets are also quite welcoming of new writers, so if you are super at creating a riveting plot line or weaving an irresistible story, look at the lists of paying markets available on **The Submission Grinder**, a free online submission-tracking tool that allows a writer to easily search for paying markets for short fiction.

The urgency of financial need has turned some very good writers into New York Times Bestselling writers. Cara Hoffman was a single mom who poured all her heart and journalistic talent into her first novel to support her son. Here's how she put it at our March 2010 salon, describing how she wrote out of financial need: "I had this great idea that to earn money to take care of the baby I would just write! [Room erupts in laughter, which she joins.] So that's what I did.... When he was two, I wrote a novel, and I just... I got a job at a newspaper. I've never written without somebody in the background being like 'La-la-la-la! Mom! Mom! Mom! Mom!'"

And when Miranda Beverly-Whittemore could not interest her publisher in a second literary novel after a critically acclaimed first, she also thought of her kids and the need for money and made a conscious decision to write a *New York Times* Bestseller, to have college savings.

Miranda related that story at a Pen Parentis Literary Salon at Andaz Wall Street in 2013, the same week that her novel *Bittersweet* hit the bestseller chart!

If writing is work, then money can be an incredible motivator... and kids are a valuable reason to make money.

A STORY FROM THE SALONS

Teresa Dzieglewicz

Teresa Dzieglewicz is an educator, Pushcart Prize-winning poet, and a co-director of the Mní Wičhóni Nakíčižiŋ Owáyawa (Defenders of the Water School) at Standing Rock Reservation.

She received her MFA from Southern Illinois University, where she received the Academy of American Poets Prize. She is the winner of the 2018 Auburn Witness Poetry Prize, and she has received fellowships from New Harmony Writer's Workshop, the Kimmel Harding Nelson Center, and the NY Mills Arts Retreat. Her poems appear or are forthcoming in the *Pushcart Prize XLII*, *Best New Poets*, *Beloit Poetry Journal*, *Ninth Letter*, *Sixth Finch*, and elsewhere.

At the time of this interview, in early 2019, her son was 7 months old and moments after we posted the interview on our website, Teresa learned she had won a Pushcart Prize in poetry.

"I would like to say that I have found the magic writing schedule for myself, but honestly, my baby's patterns are changing so much all the time that I've found I have to reshape my schedule with some frequency as well! At the moment, I generally hang out with him in the morning, and we go for a long walk that coincides with his first nap. I (ideally) use that time to brainstorm and think through my work for the day. A few times a week, I have a babysitter in the afternoon. I try to use that time fairly exclusively for writing, though I'm not often successful. Otherwise, I try to work (or clean, ugh) during his afternoon nap, and to be really present with him while he's awake. I'll put the baby to bed around 7:30, have dinner, and then sneak in a few more hours before bed. On the weekends, my husband hangs with the baby in the mornings while I write or work.

Pregnancy and parenting have opened up and enriched some new sub-set of feeling that I didn't have before (ask anyone who sat next to me as my third trimester-self sobbed through *Star Wars* of all the things). I'm near the beginning of the journey here, but I'm excited to explore what that means to me as both a writer and a human.

I read an article once that described the effect of motherhood on the brain of a rat. Before becoming a mother, the rat took her time in catching a cricket, and once it was caught, the cricket occasionally escaped. After becoming a mother, not only could the rat catch the cricket seven times as quickly, but it was never ever getting out of her claws. I have never related to any description of a creative process more. I was completing my MFA thesis during pregnancy and spent long leisurely days in the backs of coffee shops talking to myself and chasing ideas around my own brain. Now, in the hours I have to work, I am non-stop pen to paper or fingers to keys. I both appreciate and awe at my new focus and miss the meanderings of my brain. Perhaps there will be a happy medium in later stages of parenting?"

A STORY FROM THE SALONS

Wendy Chin-Tanner

Sometimes, having a child can launch a writing career. **Wendy Chin-Tanner** has two books of poetry out, *Turn* and *Anyone Will Tell You*, and is currently at work on her first novel. She is also co-author of the graphic novel *American Terrorist* and a founding editor at Kin Poetry Journal, poetry editor at *The Nervous Breakdown*, and the co-founder at *A Wave Blue World*.

This transcript from the April 2019 Pen Parentis Literary Salon relates how Chin-Tanner, a sociologist, did what she had to do to write while parenting. She is discussing her first book, which was a finalist for the Oregon Book Award in Poetry. We are at LMHQ, an event space in Lower Manhattan:

"These poems play more with form, and some of the poems are written in blank verse couplets, but the majority of them are actually written in a form that I like to call three-by-threes. They're really trisyllabic tercets that consist of three lines per stanza and three syllables per line. I developed that form when my second daughter was born and she was a marsupial baby, meaning she needed to be in a baby carrier in order to sleep. So, I would spend hours and hours everyday kind-of bounce-walking through the halls of my house. And when the insomnia unlocked the corridors of my subconscious, and I started to think of lines of poetry that I wanted to write down, all I had with me was my iPhone. And so, I opened up my iPhone Notes app, and that tiny, tiny screen kind of lends itself to really short lines. And also, because I only had one hand to type with, it was a pain in the ass to do capitalizations or commas or anything like that. So, it really, you know, the technology drove me towards—it's very pared down for that, along with the kind of kinetics of that walking—and became these 3x3 poems that have, I think, a certain musicality to them."

THE BABY YEARS

A *Summary*

Yes, everything will change. Expect it! You will have to come up with new ways to replace the resources of time, energy and money that your baby (and any additional babies!) will require.

That you picked up this book means you're ready to get back to your writing career. That's awesome. Like your baby, you'll soon be taking baby steps. Like your baby, you might fall down a lot—but just keep trying things! Use the support around you. Collect writer-parents as friends. Rely on them. You will find plenty of moms in mommy groups that will help you with stuff like how to properly get the quinoa seeds infused with the beet juice and what that does to the laundry—but make the time to collect a few mom-and-dad friends who are working on a writing or art project so that when you complain that you only finished one poem in the past six weeks, they will not say "oh wow you're a poet, I could NEVER" and instead will help you figure out where you might send it for publication!

Some creative solutions that various Pen Parentis writers have used to get more time, save money or revitalize their energy:

- *living in community with other writers to share childcare*

- *writing while baby attends an enrichment class with a spouse or a friend*

- *writing outdoors while baby naps in a stroller*

- *going to a gym that has free baby care and cutting the workout short to spend twenty minutes on writing in the gym's cafe*

- *finding a church with free childcare and writing during the service (hey, we don't endorse these solutions, we just share them!)*

- *taking turns with spouses who also write on a meticulous child-care schedule*

- *trading valuable talents (editing, writing, cleaning, cooking) for babysitting time*

- *becoming less precious about when/where you will write*

- *pooling resources to get one babysitter for two writer babies*

- *Making to-do lists for their writing tasks so when they get a random 20-Aminutes they can get something accomplished*

Getting time to yourself that you will devote to writing is important, and if you can't do that at home while baby is sleeping or otherwise occupied (when my kids were infants, I became very adept at typing while they nursed!) find other ways to grab a few minutes here and there to devote to your writing career.

You will get almost no consistent sleep at first. This will change your mental aptitude drastically. But if you are lucky enough to have enough energy to keep at the very least a journal you scribble into, the stuff you'll write in this half-awake, completely baffled, disbelieving state will be some of your most creative (even if a lot of it is incoherent) — as source material it is one step away from lucid dreaming and can be very rich. So, write when you can, but don't flog yourself if you can't.

You may find that your energy is so low that you truly can't create even a single new sentence–that's fine too. All writers have trunk stories–old ideas that can be reworked or edited into something useful. Just sit down with one of those! Tinker with words until something sparks, you're creative interest. The idea is not necessarily to come up with the next *Goon Squad* before your baby walks, it is to feed the creative side of your brain, to remind yourself you are still the person you were before you added "parent" to your special skills. Remember: "Parenting" is not a job (there is no end date to "parenthood", and you can't quit), it is a fantastic life event that will depend and enhance your perceptions of humanity. Like falling in love. Like picking up a second language. Like learning to drive. It is a moment to savor and to learn to adapt to for the rest of your life.

PART 3

Writing with a Toddler

WRITING WITH A TODDLER

Hello Little Human.

Oh, the crazy! Toddlers are endlessly inquisitive and messy. They get into everything. They leave a trail of chaos in their wake. They want to be just like you and nothing like you. They defy you just to prove they are individuals, and their remorse, like their unbridled joy, can make you giggle or weep. As they discover language, toddlers reconnect you to the language you have almost forgotten to love–it is during these years that mommy-blog posts and random midday dad tweets are the most frequent. Why not? Go for it. As a toddler, my daughter insisted on using "amn't" as a word: "I amn't hungry." She sounded like a Victorian princess. I have to admit that while I didn't document it on social media, I admired it and was loath to correct her. I desperately wanted people to know about it because it was just so clever and adorable. There were moments when I fantasized about making the phrase *amn't* famous in a meme—but really, would it have been? More likely her middle school friends would have found it with its 12 likes from other preschool-moms and teased her mercilessly. Better left un-blogged. (She tragically corrected herself around first grade... but not before I had many years of secret pleasure as she stomped her foot, furious and red-faced, declaring: "I amn't going to bed, Mommy! I amn't tired at all! You would know that if you knew me better!")

Around the age of 2, your child can no longer be mistaken for an infant, even while asleep. And once awake, you really see the difference: they don't stay where they are placed, and they clearly are developing defined notions of themselves as "other" from you. This seems as good a place as any to think about your child's right to their own story.

Who owns that story?

Writers who have kids seem to believe they must split into two categories: those who write about their kids obsessively and those who bifurcate so completely that no one even knows they have kids.

First - it's not true that only these two kinds of writers exist. This is very important. **You don't have to choose between all or nothing**. This false choice is at the heart of a lot of problems and stereotypes that writer-parents face. Every writer who has kids gets to make their own choices on how involved they will be in the child's upbringing, how much time they will spend on their own writing career, what they will write about, and whether they will or won't write about their children either directly or indirectly. It is the same choice you face in writing about your mother, your fascinating aunt Sarah, or your abusive best friend Seymour; it just takes longer for your children to recognize that you are writing about them.

There are no right answers. There are entire writing courses on memoir and motherhood. There are endless blog posts about fatherhood and children, some hilarious, some intimate and fierce. I have no answers, except to insist you reflect before publishing any personal essay. (You should do that, anyway. Your own privacy is also at stake here.) Don't get bogged down by the question but think about it. I say again, there are no right answers. There are only choices that are better or worse in your own individual situation with your own individual child. Or children. You know yourself best. Respect your own values. Make your own priorities.

There are no rules about this.

But people still sometimes fall into these two categories, so let's talk about them.

(Please be advised that I am about to talk about the extremes - not the millions of us who fall in the middle and do a little of each but hang on to our own writer-selves.)

The first extreme is those writers who obsess excessively about their kids on the page: the source is authentic. These writers understand that it is preposterous to separate who they are from their writing, but instead of rounding out who they were with the added layers of growing understanding of what it means to be a parent, they instead throw themselves headlong into writing about parenting, usually without craft: these are the writers that immediately pen trite motherhood poetry, grisly stories about their own birth process with no greater point than to complain, and embarrassing blogs about parenting that no one but their mother reads. There is nothing wrong with this sort-of writing-as-therapy, unless by doing so you are abandoning a beautiful poetry chapbook about trigonometry, a collection of well-crafted essays about forestry and the environment, or the fantastic outline of what could have been a Hugo-award winning trilogy about ancestral ghosts having tea parties. If you feel that you have to write about parenthood because that is what is expected of parents, I want to tell you to breathe easy. You don't have to start a mommy blog just because you have that material at your fingertips. At Pen Parentis, we believe you should continue to write your voice, your passions, and your subjects, whatever they are. If writing about your children is what you are called to do, then write your thing and write it truly well. Use all the elements of style and craft. If you are a new writer, take a writing class! There are online classes that work very well for new parents. But feeling that you *have* to write about being a parent because you *are* a parent is falling into the trap of stereotype.

You always have options.

Now, let's talk about the second trap: the writer who doesn't mention their child at all.

These writers have decided that the way to remain a respected writer (i.e. "cool," or replace that word with whatever current artsy phrase means the same thing: edgy, authentic, groundbreaking, enticing, experimental, cutting-edge, limitless, boundary-pushing, etc.) is to block off their parental selves, in effect divorcing their lives from their careers.

Their actions show that the stereotype they are following is not true—they have kids and are yet maintaining a successful literary career—but by hiding the fact that they are parents; they are perpetuating that stereotype for others.

These writers (often those who can afford full-time child-care, so their children can be invisible missing both from their author bios and from their author events) hide behind personal privacy. They intentionally cannot mention the fact that they are parents, secreting their (possibly even subconscious!) fears of being judged for having started a family behind an assertion that they are protecting their children. In effect, these writers deny the existence of their children, assuming their careers will be taken more seriously if they are seen as childless. Their author bios do not mention that they are parents, and when booking interviews, they announce that questions about their kids are entirely off-limits. They usually say that this is to protect their children—and while this is possible, writers (even celebrity writers) rarely have paparazzi following them around and photographing their families.

Acknowledging that an Edgar Award winner has three kids at home does not negate the award, though we acknowledge that branding has gone so far that owning up to having children might be seen as a poor marketing choice. We respect that choice, but we also fully acknowledge that hiding family from a bio is a very special, economically advantaged position to take, and one that is surprisingly harmful to economically disadvantaged peers.

If you are invited to do a public reading, and your nanny or sitter is very affordable and can stay late, then it becomes your free choice to acknowledge the fact that at home, your three-year-old incessantly draws on your laptop screen whenever you're not vigilant. You can choose to let the audience know that your appearance at the reading was at a small personal cost, or you can omit any mention of your family and concentrate only on your books and your writing. A young single mother who has no reliable support system (or no extra money to pay the sitter) does not have that same choice. If you are in *that* situation, you find it extraordinarily challenging to participate in that same reading. You would not hide the fact that you have a three-year-old—*your decision to take part* in the reading actively shows your dedication to your career, your love of writing, and your devotion to engaging in literary society.

Who is the better writer?

You can have *no idea* without reading their respective books.

Parenthood does not affect talent.

By celebrating *all* writers that have children, Pen Parentis hopes to reveal that it is economic disparity (sometimes coupled with or even replaced by extremely supportive spouses) that enables wealthier writers to hide the fact that they have kids, which fact also helps to perpetuate this myth that great writers don't have kids. If every writer who had kids were up front about having kids, we would soon discover how various writers address their need for childcare and could amass creative solutions that could work even for writers who can't afford a full-time nanny. Or in the best-case scenario, could alert philanthropists and funders that this need exists.

While money can solve some situations writer-parents face, it does not solve them all.

Let's talk about privacy in a more specific, child-centric way. We can all agree that protecting the child is a valuable goal. (I think we can all agree on that!) Since so many of us write from real life, how do we avoid stepping on our children's privacy *in our writing*?

I proposed and moderated a very popular panel at a big writer conference in 2016 in Los Angeles called "Privacy Matters: Sell Your Book, Not Your Soul." Panelists were three very successful authors who have kids and also have incredible social media followings: Mat Johnson (72.8K followers on Twitter), Mira Jacob (a cartoon panel she drew featuring her son went viral), and Miranda Beverly-Whittemore (more than a thousand likes on her author page on Facebook).

The panel discussed social media and how much personal information is too much, what sorts of posts, tweets and photos helped or hindered their book sales. The panelists all agreed that ultimately any benefit they got from exposing their children to their fans was counteracted by even the slightest negative attention. Mira's story was fascinating: her very famous graphic memoir, *Good Talk*, which was just listed in *Publishers' Weekly* top ten books to read in 2019, began from personal conversations with her own six-year-old, a half-Jewish, half-Indian son; stories which she illustrated and put on her blog. She hid his identity by naming him Z, but his lovely responses to the situations that arose as tensions from the 2016 election spread into his own family led to complicated questions, until "A Letter to my Son" explaining how Z's brown differed from Michael Jackson's brown went viral.

There is a beauty and natural humor in a parent trying to answer their son's questions honestly. And it touched the pulse of the world. The viral comic was so evocative that a publisher contacted her to request an entire memoir written in the same unique illustrated format. Mira has always been candid about the dual nature of this fame for her young son—it has had negative impact and positive. Her son was faced with issues that a celebrity child would face. Strangers knew him and commented on private matters that he thought were between him and his mother.

On the panel, Mira explained that she was always straightforward with her son and carefully listened to him, addressing each interpersonal situation as it arose. (Ultimately, her talent is unquenchable. The memoir, *Good Talk*, came out from Penguin in March 2019, to extraordinary critical acclaim, and continues to rise in fame, collecting awards and breaking ground for the graphic/illustrated memoir.)

So, your mommy blog might result in paid work—there is always that chance. Mira's straight-talking honestly and her love for her son are obvious both on the page and off. She was reluctant to put her family's personal story front and center, but the art won out. Mira is an excellent role model for how to directly write about your child while respecting their privacy.

That said, Brian Gresko, who was the curator of the Pen Parentis Literary Salons for a little over a year and who is the editor of the excellent essay anthology, *When I First Held You: 22 Critically Acclaimed Writers Talk about the Triumphs, Challenges, and Transformative Experience of Fatherhood*, began as a terrific essayist and honest writer who used his own life experience as a subject. His blog grew in popularity, but his experiences with celebrity were not as positive as Mira's. He had this to say on Babble.com in the essay "Why I've Stopped Over-Sharenting Online":

"As a writer of parenting content, I can speak of the dangers of over-sharenting first-hand.

After writing about atheism, I received a package in the mail at my home address, which included a Bible and five-page letter imploring me to accept Jesus in my heart. The author had obviously spent time reading my work, as he quoted from multiple blog posts, and referred to my son by name. This was unsettling. I lost a few nights' sleep, worried that the letter might have only been the first step, that perhaps a zealot might try to seek out my son in person. I've written his name, details about his life, even included photos of what he looks like, and the street where we live. You never know who is out there, and what an incensed reader might do.

It's affected my family on a personal level, too. I blogged with detail about my son's slow-to-develop social skills and anxiety issues, and, surprise, found playdates became hard to come by, and even family members distancing themselves because my honest, raw accounts made them uncomfortable. Sometimes people have said things to me that inspired or made their way into blog posts — some friends have been flattered; others withdrew. These have been real, tangible side-effects of my words, and while I understand that this is a peril of nonfiction writing, my relationship to my son, and my son's relationship with other people, is nothing I want to damage, or exploit."

So yes, write your blogs, your long Facebook or Instagram posts. But don't forget that whatever you put online stays forever—and while writing is still writing, blogging about your kid's milestones won't necessarily further your writing career. Brian Gresko had a difficult experience we wish on no one, and ended up struggling ultimately with the best way to end his popular blog–his followers expected to hear more and more about the child they had turned into a main character, while Brian's child was fast developing into a young person with agency. (The story ends well: Brian hosts a wildly successful reading series in Brooklyn, and running dozens of author interviews online, and is writing a novel.)

To avoid the privacy dilemma, many writers who drop anecdotes about their children into their social media or mention them in the context of a greater idea, do not use their kids' names and/or give only the vaguest descriptions. This seems healthy. It acknowledges the fact that the anecdote is funny or relatable, but it keeps the child's identity private. It allows for both worlds—you know the writer is a parent, but you don't know the details of their home life or the names of their kids.

Some writers find it easiest to deny their children altogether—big writers usually, like Jonathan Lethem, who never speaks about his own parenthood, though he often speaks of his own parents and siblings. While I understand the desire to keep your children's life private, I think it does a disservice to humanity to deny the fact that you are a parent, particularly when you are also a successful artist of the written word. People need mentors and heroes, or even just good examples, and the more big-name writers that come forth— like Stephen King and Peter Straub, proud of their writer-kids who then sometimes have their own kids—the better for that young woman in her MFA program who is wondering if it is even possible to write the great American novel and have a baby at the same time. (Answer: absolutely yes, but not easy!)

It would be great if, instead of calling up Ernest Hemmingway's tragic attitude towards fatherhood, we could all easily point to successful writers like King and Straub and Egan and yes, even Lethem, and realize that writers DO have successful careers after having kids. Need statistical proof? Nine of the last ten Nobel Prize winners in Literature were also parents!

So, when you write about your kids, you do you, but think ahead. That cute little potato is one day going to be Googling their own name. Make sure they aren't embarrassed by what they find. Not just what you write about them and their personal lives, but also what you reveal about yourself as a parent. The gleeful humor blog about the daylong spa you took as a new mom which allowed you to completely forget you had a child will surely resonate with other new moms, but in fifteen years, it could make a lonely teenager feel even more sure that you never wanted them. And remember too that while you control the content of your parenting blog, you don't control the comments that strangers make on public articles.

So, think ahead when you're writing about your kids. That's all. Take a moment to reflect before posting. Make sure you have made a conscious decision and will be happy with it long into the future. Then go for it!

A STORY FROM THE SALONS

Helen Phillips

Helen Phillips' fifth book, *The Need*, made a splash in 2019. It was a 2019 National Book Award nominee, a New York Times Notable Book of 2019, and a TIME Magazine Top 10 Fiction Book of 2019. Her short story collection Some Possible Solutions received the 2017 John Gardner Fiction Book Award. Her novel *The Beautiful Bureaucrat*, a *New York Times* Notable Book of 2015, was a finalist for the New York Public Library's Young Lions Award and the Los Angeles Times Book Prize. Her collection *And Yet They Were Happy* was named a notable collection by The Story Prize. Her children's adventure book *Here Where the Sunbeams Are Green* was published internationally as *Upside Down in the Jungle*.

Helen has received a Rona Jaffe Foundation Writer's Award, the Italo Calvino Prize in Fabulist Fiction, the Iowa Review Nonfiction Award, the DIAGRAM Innovative Fiction Award, and a Ucross Foundation residency.

Her work has been featured on Selected Shorts, at the Brooklyn Museum, and in the *Atlantic Monthly*, the *New York Times*, and *Tin House*, among others. Her books have been translated into eight languages.

A graduate of Yale and the Brooklyn College MFA program, she is an associate professor at Brooklyn College. Born and raised in Colorado, she lives in Brooklyn with her husband, artist and cartoonist Adam Douglas Thompson, and their two children.

Take heart! Helen read at Pen Parentis in 2013 and again in 2016. At the time of this interview, her son was one and her daughter was three.

"Ever since my daughter was born, I have rigorously protected an hour a day for writing. Before I became a parent, I averaged four hours a day; now it feels like a great accomplishment to carve out my one little hour. But I do find that compressing four hours' worth of creative energy into one hour has its own potency. I used to care a lot about my writing routine (where, when, what kind of tea, etc.), but now it's wherever I can do it, whenever I can do it. I always set the timer for one hour and ignore all outside demands within that time frame.

I think the most challenging thing (aside from the ever-present anxiety about the possibility of something bad happening to my children; nothing anyone tells you before you have children can prepare you for that particular brand of worry) is the nonstop quality of my life. I'm pretty much in perpetual motion from the second I wake up until the second I go to sleep, between teaching and writing and taking care of the kids and trying to prevent the apartment from descending into chaos. Sometimes, amid all that busy-ness and exhaustion, I feel a lack of connection with my inner life and I crave solitude. Reading helps, a solo walk in the park helps, a dinner out with my husband helps. Every bit of time you take for yourself comes at a literal price, but at the same time it's priceless to pay for a little extra childcare sometimes.

My main tip (for parents and non-parents alike) is to set aside a realistic amount of time each day to write, be it fifteen minutes or four hours. Be strict about honoring that time and set a timer, but within that time frame, give yourself permission to do whatever you want. Maybe it's writing down a nightmare you had or re-reading the beginning of a book you love or coming up with the stupidest first sentence you can think of—but something that keeps you connected to your creativity.

I'm still in the trenches with a baby and a toddler, but these past three years as a mother-writer have definitely given me confidence that I can continue to be a productive writer even under my new life circumstances. And the intensity of motherhood has brought a lot of urgency to my writing.

When I was pregnant with my first child, I wasted a lot of time worrying that I would stop writing once the baby was born. But in fact, writing became more important to me than ever after I became a mother. It serves as the place where I can process all the complicated emotions that come with parenthood, the bliss and the dread that very nearly defy expression, and it is my way of staying in touch with myself amid the many responsibilities in my life."

A STORY FROM THE SALONS

Mira Jacob

Mira Jacob is the author and illustrator of the critically acclaimed illustrated memoir *Good Talk: A Memoir in Conversations*. Her first book was a Barnes & Noble Discover New Writers pick, shortlisted for India's Tata First Literature Award, and long listed for the Brooklyn Literary Eagles Prize. The novel was also named one of the best books of 2014 by Kirkus Reviews, *The Boston Globe*, Goodreads, Bustle, and The Millions.

Her writing and drawings have appeared in *The New York Times*, Electric Literature, *Tin House*, Literary Hub, *Guernica*, *Vogue*, *the Telegraph*, and BuzzFeed, and she has a drawn column on ShondaLand. She teaches at The New School, and she is a founding faculty member of the MFA Program at Randolph College. She is also the Co-founder of Pete's Reading Series in Brooklyn, where she spent thirteen years bringing literary fiction, non-fiction, and poetry to Williamsburg.

She lives in Brooklyn with her husband, who is a documentary filmmaker, and their son.

She first read at a Pen Parentis Salon a little while after her first book (the moving, funny and compassionate literary novel, *Sleepwalker's Guide to*

Dancing) came out. At that time, her son was five years old. She appeared again at our Graphic Novels salon to premiere her acclaimed illustrated memoir, *Good Talk*.

Here's how Mira responded at that Salon on September 9, 2014, when asked, "So, did you write the book before you had your child or after, and how did you manage your time?"

"It took ten years.

The book was happening while I had him, and while I was running an editorial branch of a company, and while I was going through big corporate takeovers. Time management? It was a terrible story, terrible and funny and crazy.

So I was running the editorial side of a very big company that got bought out by Disney and I went into what I thought was a normal meeting and sat down with my sack of stuff, and my boss turned to me and said, "We're replacing you with five social media interns."

(The audience gasps, shocked in dismay, and Mira laughs.)

My husband is a documentary filmmaker—so we're rolling in it—so I did that thing that you do when you are an adult in the world, and you have to be normal for a certain amount of time. I said to my boss, "Ok, thank you, let me sign any documents you need," and then afterward I was walking away.

And walking down the street, I literally just took the picture of my son (from my office desk) and put it into my purse, and I started coming apart like those cartoon clocks—you know them—*sproing!* —eyeballs out to here? I started just falling apart, and I went to meet my husband under the Brooklyn Bridge, sobbing, and said, "I have ruined us. I thought that we had a safety net, but we won't have any money after two months, and I'm sorry."

At which point he did the nicest thing. He said, "You've been trying to finish this book for ten years, I think the thing you need to do is just finish the book."

It was exactly what I needed to hear.

So, I did this little alchemy in my brain (because I'm a person who worries about money a lot) and I pretended I was getting paid. And I sat down and wrote like our lives depended on it. And I finished up a book I'd been working on for ten years… in two months.

When it sold, I can tell you. There was full-body relief.

I've run a reading series for fifteen years, and I'm really aware of what the industry is like and there was a full-body relief of having it sold at all, because I know that there are so many good books that don't sell, but the biggest relief was just that….

Everything had come due. And we didn't actually have anything left. The sale just came at the exact right time. So that's how that worked out.

I'm really relieved every day. I feel like I may have used up the good luck quotient in my lifetime. But also, I feel really, sizably relieved that the book got done. The whole time I was writing it I kept thinking, "You gotta finish it for this reason, or that reason," but I didn't realize that finishing would come with such enormous relief.

And it's pretty short-lived, but it's still worth it."

WRITING WITH A TODDLER

Time

All right, so let's talk about toddlers and writing time.

Sorry to disappoint, folks, but according to all reports (and including my experience) toddlers are the most hands-on phase of childhood. For a writer, this is the actual hard part. The children at this point are so small that putting them in day care or sending them out of the house with a nanny tends to suffuse parents with guilt (don't fret, this terror is normal! Thousands and thousands of great parents have dealt with this guilt—the good thing is that if you did your parental duty, you don't *need* to feel this guilt, you just have to tolerate it when it comes. For some of you, this will be a brief flash or occasional pang, mostly because you are so happy getting back to writing that you have to set a timer to remember to pick up your kid, and for others will be a daily, painful thing complete with tears from both the child and the parent, and for some portion of you, the guilt of separation will be insurmountable and you will find another way to get your writing done.)

Feeling separation anxiety from your tiny little tot is perfectly normal! The question is, will the guilt outweigh the pleasure and relief of finally writing again?

If the answer to this is no, and you really wring your hands and waste time for several weeks in a row, then you're wasting both money and family time. Go back to your family. Try again later or find another way. Write after hours, before hours, at the playground—find space in your family time to write. Maybe if your toddler discovers the 2020 equivalent of the Wiggles or Teletubbies, you'll be able to seclude yourself at a desk for a second. Maybe your toddler will enjoy their own drawing time while their parent writes. Maybe they nap and you write during that time. Maybe you get a sitter every so often or your spouse steps up to give you two hours on Saturday mornings. Maybe your mother wants some grandma time. Maybe toddler bedtime is early enough that you still have some creative energy left in you once a week and you can get away from Netflix to write a new poem. Find your way.

Most parents of toddlers eventually get over the guilt of separation because the pleasure of returning to some kind of writing routine is so considerable. Sending out your first new piece after having a baby should result in a huge celebration, because it truly is a milestone.

But if you don't have time for that—you are not alone. Make sure you do something, anything, with your great ideas. Jot them down. Our members have used napkins, bar coasters, diaper boxes, paper, and yes, lots of technology (any app that allows you to speak directly into the phone to transcribe is a big hit with most of the parents who use it!) The important thing here is not to lose the idea in the clatter and clutter of 24/7 parenting. You can always make a file of "ideas for later" and go back to it when your kids start kindergarten.

Toddlers eventually give up their naps (unless you are truly lucky) and some of them wake excruciatingly early or refuse to go to bed. These are parenting issues that would be difficult even if you weren't trying to carve out time to write. It's okay. If you have a spouse or partner, enlist their help to give you some child-free time. If you don't, you can hire help. If you can't do that, consider enrichment classes that are drop off and covet those 45 minutes for your writing. If you can't afford any of this, find a friend who also has a similar-aged kid, and try trading one day per week of a few hours of playdate. Remember that the barter system is alive and well - you might be able to trade your fantastic lasagna once per week for two hours of childcare from a friend who hates to cook but is great with your kid. You're a creative human being. Think outside the box.

The goal is to get some kind of regular writing time into your schedule during the years that your kid is little and on-the-move—from age 2-5; it is difficult but not impossible to find time to write. Maybe a better way to think of it is that during this time, you're going to have to MAKE time to write.

Let me give you some examples of how other writers have found (or made) time to write during this most challenging writing time of your parenting life.

- Writing before the kids are up

- Writing after the kids go to bed (most common by FAR)

- Waking up at 4am and writing for an hour, then sleeping again (I know!!)

- Hiring a nanny to watch the kids 1xweek after school while you go to a coffee shop

- Hiring a teenager to watch kids in the house while you write in a "no entry" room

- Hiding in a closet (yes, really)

- Hiding in a bathroom (not joking, these are real stories)

- Taking turns with spouse or another writer on a strictly maintained "fair" schedule

- Writing in a nearby cafe or library during drop-off playdates

- Writing in the lobby of an hour-long class (gymnastics, music, language)

- Writing while the kids are in a religious class

- Writing while the kids watch TV or iPad (I'm not condoning, just reporting!)

- Getting kids to write while you write (anyone who manages this is a miracle worker!)

- Writing at the playground while the kids play

- Taking a "writing retreat" in a nearby hotel—one writer did this for several months every other weekend to finish her novel, she said it worked better for her than a residency or colony because it was solitary and close enough that if there were actual emergencies she could come home, plus she saved herself the time and effort of filling out applications

- Taking a writing retreat at grandma's house (you have to have a good relationship with parents/in-laws for this to work, since you won't be available to hang out or chat)

- Writing on the subway or bus to and from preschool pickups (only works in urban centers, obviously)

As you can see, it's pretty random and all over the place. Somehow, toddlers can always sense that you are in the house, particularly if you are focusing on something other than them. They come seek out their parents to see what they're doing. Particularly when the writing is either going extremely well, or very badly, it's quite hard not to be annoyed at the interruptions. If you plan ahead and really remove yourself from the house, it will go better for your writing (and make you less angry at your kid for just being loving and wanting attention!)

WRITING WITH A TODDLER

Energy

Another thing that can be very discouraging in the toddler years is how much actual energy it takes to parent a toddler. They are constantly on the go, they rarely are obedient listeners (around age 2 they have to separate from their parents, so they start being quite defiant. In my experience, humorous reverse psychology worked wonders during this time, but my kids were game for being told "don't you dare eat that piece of broccoli" and that's just my house - you will find your own way through this thorny time period). What will definitely happen, though, is at the end of every full-time day with a toddler, you are going to be sapped for energy.

Even if you have an hour or two after Junior's bedtime and before you need to turn in, you'll be very lucky to feel the emotional creativity to write a new story or delve into the psychological thriller you were writing before Junior was born. A lot of mommy blogs are born during the toddler years. It is fun to catalogue the day's events, to complain to an online group, to make sense out of impossible happenings, to share funny stories of misspoken words and new discoveries. Remember that mommy blogs are temporary— very few careers are born of mommy blogs. Better for your writing career if you can spend a few minutes editing an old story, researching colonies that give extra money to writers who need child care or residencies where you can bring your child (there are a few, and more programs are added every year as the Sustainable Arts Foundation funds organizations that make it easier for parents to continue to be artists and writers).

Some writers take to getting up early to write during toddler years because their energy is so low by the end of the day that they retrain themselves to think in the morning - even if they used to be night-writers. Other writers discover that their toddler magically knows when they wake, and it only makes their child wake earlier. The biggest obstacle is often how to get started—many writers completely abandon their routines when a newborn was introduced into the home, and once the baby is a toddler, they find there just isn't any time to get started. Here are five ways to get yourself over the hurdle to actually jump in and begin something new and daunting:

1) ASSESS: take some time to canvass your writing situation. What is going to be hard? Do you have a good writing space? Can you carve out a few hours? What project do you want to work on? Will it require research? How long is it likely to take? Do you need to install writing software, or password protect your laptop? Do you have a great way to back up work? Toddlers can easily spill your necessary caffeinated beverage all over that laptop - getting a program that automatically backs up to the cloud might be the best investment you make! Take that time to think and figure out what you believe the pitfalls might be. But also look at the strengths. You love the project. The ideas need to be out in the world. You love to write. You just repainted your home office and the sage blends perfectly with the white curtains and you can't wait to spend ten minutes alone in here with a cup of tea... anything to motivate you.

2) COMPARE: find an example of someone who has already done this. Visit the Pen Parentis website, for example, and check out the interviews we have posted with other writer-parents. Read a blog about writing while

parenting (Cari Luna, who read at Pen Parentis and is a longtime supporter of our work, has a wonderful blog called "Writer, with Kids" that she no longer adds to, but the archive is available online.) There are new groups on social media all the time: WriterMomsInc is a Facebook group for new moms that mostly has emerging writers that started fiction careers after having their first baby. Google is your friend here. Find the other parent writers in the world and see how they did it. Get inspired. Steal their tips and ideas. Always ask for what you need—post in a group forum if you are stuck. People have done what you are doing. At Pen Parentis Salons, for example, we never tell you what you should be doing. We tell you it absolutely can be done - we know, because everyone we present has done it. So, find yourself some mentors or idols who went through what you are going through now and then take some time to figure out how their methods can be modified to work for you.

3) DO THE EASY STUFF: pick the part of starting that takes no energy. Do you love to tidy up? Clean your desktop so it is ready for you to start tomorrow... or the day after... Do you love to research? Get that spreadsheet started. Write the first sentence or a one-line plot summary depending if you're a Panster or Plotter (one who writes by the seat of their pants or one who writes from an outline) Start small. Get something accomplished. One sentence. One word. Just name a file on your desktop. Just do something.

4) FACE FACTS: don't hide from the obstacles you are going to face. Does your spouse think writing is a stupid hobby and a waste of your precious parenting time? Do they think you need to make some money to support Junior? Does your kid have special needs that make all this advice sound like "let them eat cake"? Face these obstacles head on. Make a list. Figure out what is going to make it hard for YOU to get through your writing project. Putting it all on paper (or screen) will at least make you stop hitting

walls. You'll know what you need to face, and you can set up a plan for each item. Some might be impossible. That's fine—we do the impossible all the time as parents. Don't worry - you've got this.

5) MAKE A PLAN: phase out the work. Can you make an outline by next month? Can you write 500 words by the end of the week? Break the project down into manageable goals and write them all out. Even if you don't keep to your timeline, knowing what the entire project will look like beginning to end will give you tangible goals.

WRITING WITH A TODDLER

Money

You know that saying that goldfish will grow only to the size of their tank? It's a myth—goldfish are indeterminate growers and if they are healthy, they will continue to grow until they die.

Similarly, a child will cost whatever amount you are willing to spend. No joke. Fantastic adults have been raised at sub-poverty level (Stephanie Zhou, Dr. Khumar Bahuleyan) and fantastic adults have been raised in the lap of luxury (Georgina Bloomberg, Azim Premji). In parenting, there is no guarantee that throwing money at a problem will definitely solve it. That said, throwing money at a problem can often help - there are plenty of experts out there charging $150-500/hour for everything from sleeping through the night, obedience training, allergy proofing your house, organic food classes, music, dance, art, languages, play-care, socializing, math, STEM—there is no end to the enrichment possibilities for your not-yet-entirely verbal toddler.

Like on your wedding, you can blow the bank, or you can elope. Or you can opt out entirely. It's up to you.

When a sitter re-negs at the last minute or flakes out and doesn't show at all, should that parent skip the reading? Bring the child? It is a quandary that many of our readers have faced! Readings help book sales, and they are often paid events. They are a fantastic way to build your audience and to create lifelong fans of your writing. But at $15/hour (much higher in NYC, and exorbitant if you use a last-minute sitting bonded service) hiring a babysitter will negate most of your income and publicity gain.

Specific to writing, it can be emotionally hard to do readings. Even if you have no guilt about leaving your tiny tot with a sitter, they often throw impressive tantrums at this age. Imagine how it feels when you are *not* a parent and arrive to do a small bookstore reading where only three people have showed up in the rain—and now imagine the same three-person turn-out when you are walking away from a sobbing toddler and know you will be paying someone $15/hour at the end of the night.

Finding sitters who are reliable is not easy. Leaving toddlers with sitters at night isn't for everyone. Not all new parents have supportive spouses. There can be tricky conversations about finances that reduce the benefit of public readings to immediate book sales, so that instead of a cheerful "how was the audience," after an event, some spouses demand accounting: "How many books did you sell?"

What a way to crush a writer's spirit and turn them into a marketing tool.

I'm not advocating bringing your child to work, but by not mentioning that you have them at all, it perpetuates this myth that successful artists have no kids. Why do writers feel they have to hide their children? — Having kids is part of life. Not everyone is wealthy enough to grab a sitter and pop out for four hours on a week's notice or to take a month away for a Yaddo residency, but wouldn't it be nice if instead of asking interviewers not to talk about their kids at all, all writers who are parents could publicly admit the means by which they kept that writing career on track.

Wouldn't that be an interesting change?

There are no guarantees. Do what is best for your child. Do take a parent-finance class if you can find one (again, you can pay for this or find one for free on YouTube or at your local library or community center). Money for kids is generally a long-term goal, and not everyone can manage.

Toddlers are the kids that are just as happy playing with boxes as they are with the incredible gizmos that came inside those boxes. Remember that too, creativity is often born of need. (Think of the raven who can't get the berry floating on the water deep in the vase, so fills the vase with stones until the water rises enough that the berry floats near the top.)

Don't worry too much. Be reasonable. Know your own needs and your own capabilities. There will ALWAYS be people who do more than you and people who do less. Don't try to be anyone but yourself.

There are a few scholarships and fellowships available for parents of young children who are writers in addition to the usual grants available to all writers. Search engines are your friend - find the opportunities that are right for you.

Pen Parentis offers an annual Writing Fellowship for New Parents. It is not enough money to allow you to quit everything and just write your novel, but our goal isn't to support a writer-parent for a year, our goal with this fellowship is to encourage the production of new works at a time that is critical to writers who have kids. We offer $1000 to a writer who parents a child under 10 years old. We want you to write something new each year. We want to get you to reconnect with your creativity, to prove to yourself you can do it. Other organizations give more money — Sustainable Arts Foundation comes to mind. Their individual grants for writers and artists are substantial, and their application is not onerous. We encourage all writing parents to apply for their fellowship. And as in all things, if you don't succeed the first time, don't give up! You'd tell your kid to try again - take your own advice.

When sending out short stories and articles, start with paying markets. Make yourself a list of highest-paying to lowest that are looking for the thing you write - and go down in that order. Why not? You might be rejected by your top four, but had you gone from the bottom up, the fourth market likely would not have paid you at all!

Short fiction, poems, articles - these can be sold. Learn to pitch if you are good at nonfiction. Develop relationships with editors in paying markets in journals that cover the sort of thing you are happy to write about. Be aware, however, that writing a column or a blog that makes money swiftly overtakes your urge to write the great sci-fi novel of all time. Make sure you save some energy and time to devote to the book you'd love to write. It won't write itself.

Grants are a great idea - many states have grants for writers, and although the application is tedious and requires a great deal of detail-oriented work, once you've done it, you can tweak it every year and hopefully win a grant.

Just in case you're not up on these things:

GRANTS: money you are expected to spend on a certain thing. There are grants for particular writing projects (like a particular novel or story collection, or writing about a certain subject) and there are grants for certain kinds of people (many diversity grants are available and most ethnic groups have at least one grant available, religions sometimes offer money for writing, as do many other subjects: science, art, history, gender studies...) Grants are not usually quick money - they are a large lump payment and sometimes come with the requirement that you explain how you use the money towards the project.

FELLOWSHIPS: this money is for a person, not necessarily for a project. Often there is a residency requirement or work aspect connected to the money. Universities and Colonies often have fellowships. Guggenheim Fellowships are the most famous. People who have all won the same Fellowship are often called "alumni" of the Fellowship. Or Former Fellows.

(But in our case, Pen Parentis Fellows are fellows forever! We love to see what they do and keep in touch with them as much as possible.)

SCHOLARSHIPS: this is money devoted to you being able to attend a particular course of study or event—writing workshops sometimes give scholarships, universities do, classes. These are often need-based.

The best part is that none of these three things have to be repaid. You do have to pay taxes on all three; they are income. But still - they're amazing to win, because there is honor attached to each one. It is a selection process and your talent levels influence the choice.

So, don't give up. There is money out there for writers. Find it. Apply for it. Hone your skills and work hard to always improve. Good luck.

A STORY FROM THE SALONS

Elisa Albert

Elisa Albert is the author of After Birth (2015), The Book of Dahlia (2008), How This Night is Different (2006), and the editor of the anthology Freud's Blind Spot (2010). Her fiction and nonfiction have appeared in Tin House, The New York Times, Post Road, The Guardian, Gulf Coast, Commentary, Salon, Tablet, Los Angeles Review of Books, The Believer, The Rumpus, Time Magazine, on NPR, and in many anthologies. Albert grew up in Los Angeles and received her MFA from Columbia University, where she was a Lini Mazumdar Fellow.

A recipient of the Moment magazine emerging writer award and a finalist for the Sami Rohr Prize for Jewish Literature, she has received residencies and fellowships from The Virginia Center for Creative Arts, Djerassi, Vermont Studio Center, The Netherlands Institute for Advanced Studies in Holland, the HWK in Germany, and the Amsterdam Writer's Residency. She has taught at Columbia's School of the Arts, The College of Saint Rose, and was Visiting Writer at Bennington College.

This quote is from a 2016 interview for the Pen Parentis Research Project.

"Raising young kids is all-consuming, so cut yourself a break and don't make yourself (or them!) miserable by hyperventilating about your professional status (or lack thereof). It's like a decade and a half before your kids are like: please leave me alone, right? And hopefully creative fertility is forever.

So, relax, you'll have plenty of time to put pedal to the metal, ambition-wise."

THE TODDLER YEARS

A *Summary*

These few years will probably be the hardest you have to face, if all goes well. Toddlers are autopilot id-machines and they need (or at least want) you pretty much all the time they are awake. They are busy; they are curious; they notice if you are distracted, they want to be watched constantly. Plus, they'll be toilet training and there's nothing like cleaning excrement to make you feel mired in graphic domesticity.

Plus, you'll still be tired because (sorry) most toddlers wake before dawn and almost all of them have this uncanny knowledge for when their parents are also awake—even if these parental units are off in another room.

It's not a great time to tackle a six-part novel in an alternate universe - unless you have great childcare and zero guilt—but if that's the case, why are you reading this book? Go write your novel, you, lucky soul who might also be a sociopath.

ANYWAY.

The great part is, toddlers are hilarious, they see the world as a magical place, and if you pay attention, they show you the world through their eyes. It isn't long before they become little kids and are delighted to have playdates and be left with (friendly, vetted) babysitters.

Writing advice for the toddler years? Hang in there! Write short things! Do what you can!

PART 4

Writing with A Little Kid

WRITING WITH A LITTLE KID

Time

Get ready to wake up one morning and discover you have more than an hour to yourself. Well, first you will lose your mind trying to explain to Junior and Junior Miss that they need to both get their shoes on, that pajamas are not school-appropriate clothing, that the homework they are waving at you was meant to be done the night before, that you don't know where their library book is (that is their responsibility), that they both forgot to feed the dog and what? There is a Math Celebration at 9am? But that is only thirty-five minutes after drop-off, and what are you supposed to do for that amount of time?

The answer? Coffee shops.

(Pen Parentis has, incidentally, developed an app with the help of the Pace University Seidenberg School of Computer Science to track the time you write in tiny increments and add it up - so that if you happened to spend that thirty-five minutes crafting the second half of a sentence that has been plaguing you, you can add it to the three minutes you spent while waiting for Junior to run back and get the soccer ball he forgot in the class-room and the ten minutes you spent waiting for Junior Miss to change out of the bathing suit top and into something school-appropriate.)

Despite the math celebrations, the class parent meetings, the PTA meetings, the history presentations, the science fairs, and the full-grade

ELA Publication parties, you will still have more time to yourself than you have had in the entire toddler and infancy of your child(ren). Also? You will be decently well rested.

Even if you hold a full-time job, the problems that will confront you will be small potatoes next to what you've been through (the fevers, the rashes, the bumped heads and split lips, the insane poop, the sleepless hallucinations) and those that are still ahead (drugs, sex, teenage screen time, scary friends, school pressure). This is the time of friend-drama and playdates.

Obviously, special needs kids will have their needs.
Obviously, people with four or five kids will go through all this piecemeal.
Obviously, some people will have it harder.

That is always the way. But first grade through fifth grade is a sort-of parenting plateau. If you can reconnect with your former self now. Remember what you used to like to write and make a reentry. Dabble in your own creativity. Try something new. Short form creative writing is positively made for this time period in your life. Finish short fiction you began while the baby was small or that you abandoned after having a child. Go back to it. Find your voice. For the next five or so years, you will be able to develop a routine for writing. Do this! Yes, you'll have some interference with school and family obligations, yes, sometimes there will be a bad stomach flu and you'll lose 24 hours while you nurse Junior back to health, and then another 24 hours of feeling like death yourself. Yes, there will be meetings with teachers and bosses, and there will be plenty of chaos. That's life. It is no different from your childless colleagues who have to take their dog to the vet or who have aging parents to care for. We all have distractions.

But right now - time is yours to begin to repossess. Take it in small doses. But take it.

A STORY FROM THE SALONS

Patty Dann

Patty Dann is the author of *The Butterfly Hours: Transforming Memories into Memoir*, *The Goldfish Went on Vacation: A Memoir of Loss* and *The Baby Boat: A Memoir of Adoption*. She has also published four novels, *Mermaids*, *Starfish*, *Sweet & Crazy*, *and The Wright Sister*. Her work has been translated into French, German, Italian, Portuguese, Dutch, Chinese, Korean and Japanese. Her novel *Mermaids* was made into a movie, starring Cher, Winona Ryder and Christina Ricci.

Her articles have appeared in *The New York Times*, *The Boston Globe*, *The Chicago Tribune*, *The Philadelphia Inquirer*, *The Christian Science Monitor*, *O Magazine*, *The Oregon Quarterly*, *Redbook*, *More*, *Forbes Woman*, *Poets & Writers Magazine*, *The Writer's Handbook*, *Dirt: The Quirks, Habits and Passions of Keeping House* and *This I Believe: On Motherhood*.

She has served as a judge for the Scholastic Young Writers Awards. She has an MFA in Writing from Columbia University and a B.A. from the University of Oregon. Dann has taught at Sarah Lawrence Writing Institute, and the West Side YMCA and was cited by New York Magazine as one of the "Great Teachers of NYC." 2007 Book of the Year for Writing About Family and Relations from ForeWord Magazine for *The Goldfish Went on Vacation.*

When she read at Pen Parentis in February 2018, many of her former students showed up to let her know she had transformed their lives.

"I live in NYC, where I raised my son. I have written since college, while working at the A&E TV Network, publishing houses and magazines. I now teach writing workshops at the West Side YMCA. My first husband died when my son was 4 years old. I have since remarried and have two stepsons.

For me, becoming a parent and then quickly becoming a widow are so intertwined. Being a widow with a four-year-old child was exhausting and wonderful and exciting and excruciating. I and my son quickly found comfort with other widows and children, 9/11 widows, and widows who died from accidents and illness as my husband did. There were no rules. We did the best we could. When my son was young, he once said, "all you do is type on your stupid computer."

My mother was a writer, and when she typed endlessly on her typewriter, I felt left out.

I prefer writing in the morning but work and life often intervene. When I started writing I was very particular about where and when I wrote. First adopting my son and then becoming a widow three years later, made me a more flexible person and have learned to write at all hours of the day and night. I've been to writers' colonies, but I don't need that. I like to write at home and often listen to classical music when I write.

Being a parent has made me open to all kinds of conversations with grownups and children that I never had before. I often have used the dialogue of children in my writing, both fiction and non-fiction. When my son was young, I never thought of it being awesome to be a writer. I was often overwhelmed, but now I realize what a remarkable time it was."

A STORY FROM THE SALONS

Will Chancellor

Will Chancellor is the author of A *Brave Man, Seven Storeys Tall*. His essays, profiles and criticism have appeared in Bookforum, *Interview Magazine*, BuzzFeed, Literary Hub, Electric Literature, and *The White Review*, among other places. He grew up in Hawaii and Texas and teaches high school and college courses to students in Europe and the Middle East.

We asked him how he deals with maintaining the energy to write - his daughter was five years old at the time of this interview.

"There are two novelists with children who let me vent. My boss is incredibly supportive. My mom flies in from Texas to stay with my daughter when I need to travel for writing.

(I work on) Eradicating any trace of preciousness from my conception of the writing process.

Books are written in scraps when you have big real-world responsibilities at work and at home. I literally wrote the first draft of my first book on a scroll of vellum in a house in the woods. Now I'm writing on the back of credit card receipts and on the Notes app of my phone.

I'm inside a much bigger life now. There's a tendency among writers to be dangerously free, to skate around reality. Parents can't do that. Frost has a line I like a lot, "The best way out is always through." To me, this means rather than avoid responsibility with a life in books, you have to confront Time and the reality that you are a small, small part of a bigger world, which is also the world you must lead your child through."

WRITING WITH A LITTLE KID

Energy

Get happy - you will also have more energy during this time! Sleep and food routines will become fairly normalized and therefore you will know when your free time is: whether it is early mornings before the family wakes, or while children are at school, or while (There will be the outliers among you who have kids whose allergies you can't figure out, or who are single parenting, or have spouses with different hours than yours, or who have multiple kids or loud neighbors, or who have decided to parent in an unusual way that will wreak havoc on your own schedule but will ultimately result in a cool adult you raised—you know who you are, don't complain you don't have time to write, you've got other priorities. Write when you can.)

This is a window of relatively stable schedules, at least during school hours (and: if you are wealthy, or urban, or particularly industrious, or just that desperate) also of copious after-school activities. There are hours when your kids are not home. Nights are also relatively routine—a bedtime will be established and mostly kept. There will be some negotiation on how to use that time if there is a spouse involved—how much writing time do you need? How much do you actually want? But supportive partners and families have enabled writers to finish entire novels during this period of the child's life.

WRITING WITH A LITTLE KID

Money

Oh money. Freakin' money. Okay—so if you are not sending your child to private school, you are no longer spending the enormous sums that Montessori, or your lovely nanny, or copious babysitters and diapers, cost. (If you are sending your child to private school, you can just skip the money chapter altogether. I'm sure you've got your 501k in order and a 509 plan and a college fund. The rest of you panic now, it will keep you from panicking later. Have lots of awkward conversations in which you have to defend a career that pays only AFTER the work is done, and even then, not copiously or fairly. We aren't writers for the money.)

There are still babysitters and enrichment activities, both of which will cost a lot more than you expect and feel much more vital than you ever thought they would. It's okay. Just do what you have to do.

However, once you've decided that yes, writing is what you want, and you have either gotten a day job or a teaching gig to help with the bills, or made a spousal arrangement whereby it is okay that you are not earning as much as your spouse (or maybe you are!) and you are really ready to write—let me give you some lovely places to get money:

State Grants. Google your state and "writing grant"—most states have money to offer to writing projects. New York has a terrific grant for $7,000 of unrestricted funds.

Sustainable Arts Foundation. Each year, they award twenty grants of $5,000 to a parent who is also a writer. (They also fund visual artists and various multimedia people—check out their website for details)

Pen Parentis. We award a $1,000 Fellowship that comes with publication, a public reading, and a year of mentorship to one talented writer who has a child under ten years old.

NEA. If you can stomach the application, the National Endowment for the Arts has a lot of money for writers. The application might kill you, though. Maybe only Virgos should apply for this. (Just kidding. Sort of.)

But really, there are so many more. This is the website I check when I need money:

https://fundsforwriters.com/grants/

This is only a list of grants. Another common way writers supplement their income while writing a novel is to get a day job (preferably one that doesn't require you to write so you still have a lot of creative energy—or better still one in which you are free to write while on the job and that offers medical benefits)—teaching is probably what most writers do, though editing comes close second; but if you talk to many writers who are teachers, they will often tell you they have to take an actual vacation or sabbatical to have the energy to write—and when you have little kids, it is hard to take a vacation or sabbatical without them! So, make sure to consider your own writing time if/ when you take a teaching job. It is perfectly valid to go into work one hour early to write (if you have an office) or to set up camp in the school's library or other quiet corner for a solid hour before your classroom day begins.

Ghostwriting is lucrative, but again, be careful that you aren't spending every fiber of your creative energy on this high-pressure job. Ghostwriting includes many variables: there is a team demanding you meet deadlines, there is a voice that you have to match, there are the personalities involved (clients are always somehow irritating, whether they refuse to respond to emails, or whether they want you to change everything fifty times, or whether they want you to simper about following them on their routines to "really get them") — but friends, there is plenty 'o' money in ghostwriting, and if you can write a book or two a year, you can make a pretty penny—you just need to again make sure you don't drain your own creative juices in the service of money.

Well, that's probably the message of this entire section: earn the money in whatever way you must but save some time and energy for your personal creativity. I know writers who run writing groups because this is the only way they can hold themselves accountable to create.

In short, money is out there—you can pay your bills and still write your novel on the side.

And then, well, you can always, you know, sell your book.

Or a short story.

Or a poem.

Or win a contest.

None of these things will likely pay your rent (except maybe selling your book). But they will make you feel so good you'll be happy to go to your day job the next day and the next.

Incidentally, you can also write while commuting: Sean Farrell wrote the entire first draft of *The Man in the Empty Suit*, I repeat, wrote an entire time-traveling, multiple-selves-at-a-party novel while taking the subway the hour to and from his day job and his very distant apartment. He wrote the entire book on his PHONE. (His book, incidentally, is fantastic, if you have the mental energy to wrap your mind around time travel this way.)

A STORY FROM THE SALONS

Scott Nadelson

Scott Nadelson is the author of six books, most recently the novel *The Fourth Corner of the World*. He is the winner of the Reform Judaism Fiction Prize, the Great Lakes Colleges New Writers Award, and an Oregon Book Award, and teaches at Willamette University and in the Rainier Writing Workshop MFA Program at Pacific Lutheran University.

He read at Pen Parentis in 2015. He lives in Salem, Oregon, with his wife, the artist Alexandra Opie—their daughter was five and a half at the time of this interview.

"In the baby days I walked around in a fog of exhaustion so all-encompassing that it induced its own sort of dream state, which made for some interesting writing. Now that parenting demands have changed from purely physical to mostly emotional, I find myself having to work harder to get into that dream-state of story—it takes more effort to let go of the daily demands of work and family and feel free to play in the world of make-believe. But I'm also more amazed by the daily experience, watching my daughter coming into her own as a feisty little person, whose favorite band at the moment (a source of great pride for me) is The Talking Heads.

I wish I'd always known, even before I became a parent, that I could find a way to write no matter the circumstances. I used to think I needed at least three hours, absolute quiet, my coffee mug just so on the desk... After my daughter was born, it took me a few months to understand that I can always find time, and I can be far more efficient than I used to be. Now if I have fifteen minutes between meetings, in a crowded coffee shop, I can get something down on paper. And I'm so much more grateful for the time that I do have that even if I don't get anywhere with the work, as long as I'm enjoying myself, I never feel that I've squandered it.

Mostly I'd advise parent writers—or any writers—to remember what gives them joy, and to seek that out every time they sit down to write. The best piece of advice I've ever heard came from Grace Paley, who knew something about balancing work and life; she told a teacher of mine, when he was whining about how badly his writing was going, "So quit if you don't like doing it. No one cares whether you write or not." Of course, no one cares as much as we do about our own writing—so if we're going to do it, we may as well have as much fun as possible. Don't waste a minute on anything you're writing because you feel you should be writing it; write only because you want to, because you love to, because you need to.

One last thing: what I've learned above all, is that while writing is hard, it's a snap compared to parenting. You can fail at writing, and nothing is really at stake. But being a parent gives you all sorts of practice with things you inevitably deal with in writing: constant surprises, emotional swings, incredible vulnerability. Everything you need to write well; you can probably learn by parenting."

A STORY FROM THE SALONS

Catherine Parker Edmonson

Catherine Parker Edmonson is an art historian who studies interwar Paris's role as a crucible for cross-genre creative work. While she has never read at Pen Parentis, she has been a loyal Pen Parentis title member for many years, supporting our work in New York City from her home in a small college town in Mississippi. In 2018, Pen Parentis awarded her a registration to a large writing conference, where she first got to know us in person. During the COVID-19 quarantine in early 2020, she joined our National Writer-Parents Meetup. Edmonson found the group's weekly accountability sessions allowed her to make significant strides on the novel she worked on for years. A stolen painting, repatriation ethics and a deserted house in New Orleans are at the heart of this novel-in-progress, which is informed by her past work with Christie's Auctions in New York City.

This is her response to the question: how have your children influenced your writing? At the time of this writing epiphany, her kids were 2 1/2 and 4.

"Proofing a draft of my novel, one chapter caught my attention. It was shorter than the others. More fun, too. It clipped along, speedy, crisp.

What made this chapter so different?

Looking at my calendar, I realized I'd written it while home with sick kids. For three days, I'd had almost no bandwidth. My reality smelled of bleach. My kids had a stomach flu and were unpredictably demanding. And what I wrote was good. Good!

The scene I turned out was set in São Paulo's swanky Itaim Bibi neighborhood, where my protagonist confronts her blackmailer.

Immersing myself in the story, and in memories of a work trip to Brazil, bolstered my strength. Writing was a refreshing escape.

While doing laundry or emptying trash cans, I ruminated on my naughty protagonist's hijinks. Was she dining at Figueira Rubaiyat, a restaurant built around a giant Bengal fig tree? What tantalizing adjectives best describe the fresh passion fruit juice?

Having only very brief periods to write compressed the chapter; I had a story to get down and only short bursts to do it. Digressing wasn't an option. The chapter I produced stood apart from my other writing. Moving forward with my novel, I aim to apply this lesson and produce exclusively compact chapters. Sans sick kids."

THE LITTLE KID YEARS

A *Summary*

If all is typical, this is the first time you have good sleep, enough time, and some few hours away from your child to yourself. The hard part during these years is facing the guilt: we did a survey (see the Snack Jar for more on the writer-parent survey conducted by Mary Harpin on our behalf) of about 150 writers who had kids of various ages and 100% of the moms and most of the dads mentioned GUILT as a factor that kept them from writing as much as they wanted.

So okay: forgive yourselves, writers.

We were all people before we had kids, and as people we need stuff.

If you are a writer, you inherently need to write. It's a fact. Writers just do.

In these years, you are likely to get some kind of childcare, whether it is daycare, a nanny, or just a friend or family member willing to watch your kid for a little while. And at some point, your kid is going to start school. This means you can build a new writing routine, if you wish. It can be as frequent as a daily hour, or a one-per-week writing block, or even an annual week away, if you have people you trust to watch your children. There are an increasing number of parent-friendly writing residencies and some of them allow you to bring your child and some will give you extra money to pay for childcare, and a few sole heroic ones have activities for your kids while you are writing. Pen Parentis has a list of these online at **writerparentannex.com**.

> *But it all boils down to: what do you want to write and how badly do you want to write it?*

PART 5

Writing with A Big Kid

WRITING WITH A BIG KID

Time

I wasn't sure if I should separate the middle-school years, but I decided that it really is different from having a kid beginning elementary school or in kindergarten. By now, your kids are much more independent. They may transport themselves to and from school on bikes or walking, or at least you have (hopefully) come up with some carpools to lessen the burden of being a constant taxi for your child. In New York City, where I raised my two kids, middle school is when the Department of Education issues student metro cards with three free daily trips, allowing a kid to go to school, take themselves to an after-school activity or friend's house, and then come back home—all on their own.

Your kids' social lives will ramp up in middle school. There are copious sleepovers and playdates with middle-school friends, and their after-school activities are plentiful, and become important to them. The internet will become an issue, whether friend or foe. In middle school, your kids are becoming little individuals with very strong opinions and trying to run their own schedules. You will have a lot more time to yourself, but when they want your attention, they will get it—they will text you if they have phones, they will shout for your attention from all over the house (even if that is against the rules), they will want you when they want you and this will have nothing to do with your own convenience. Kids are naturally very self-centered as pre-teens and early teens, and while this is an ordinary phase of their development, it can be so grating when you have told them you're going to need one hour to work on your novel without interruption and then five minute in, they slip you a note asking if they can have a friend over. With girls there will be emotional drama over whether other girls are friends or foes. (My suggestion, just nod and smile and let the whole drama wash over you like a poison bath.... but you do you.) With boys there is the constant struggle with screen time and how much is too much (and the added joy of trying to determine whether the in-game friends they are making online (who are 24 and live in Sweden and Japan are nice people or threats). In other words, while time management will be easier, emotional situations as a parent will be harder—which can in its way impinge on your writing time, depending on whether you can turn off your natural parental anxiety or not.

But timewise, you will finally catch a break. There are fewer classroom "math celebrations" or "poetry parties" during middle school and fewer opportunities to volunteer (oh don't you worry, if you are clamoring to volunteer, there are plenty of Snowballs and Soccer Parties that you can still take on).

Middle school means established routines. The schools are trying to teach your kids to be more organized, and so most of their activities will be set in stone. The homework will be clear. Doesn't mean it will be easy, but at least in the realm of time management, you should be able to find some stability and set up routines for your own writing time.

Middle school is when stay-at-home parents return to their abandoned full time or part-time corporate jobs again. This is also when many long-abandoned novels get published. This is when Jennifer Egan won her Pulitzer Prize. She had to make a soccer-championship analogy before her two sons properly understood how amazing her achievement was. Just saying.

A STORY FROM THE SALONS

Daphne Uviller

Daphne Uviller is the author of the novels *Wife of the Day*, *Hotel No Tell*, and *Super in the City—the Zephyr Zuckerman series*—which were optioned for television by Paramount Pictures and Silver Lake Entertainment. She is also the Co-editor of the anthology *Only Child: Writers on the Singular Joys and Solitary Sorrows of Growing Up Solo*. She is a former Books and Poetry editor at *Time Out New York*, and her reviews, profiles, and articles have been published in *The Washington Post*, *The New York Times*, *Newsday*, *The Forward*, *New York Magazine*, *Allure*, and *Self*, for which she wrote an ethics column. She lives in Sleepy Hollow, NY with one husband, one dog, and two children.

This interview was conducted for our online interview series, about a year after she read at Pen Parentis.

"My daughter, a sixth grader--we just landed on Planet Middle School this year—is 11 going on 27. I know everyone says that about some girls, but really, everyone says that about her. More than two people (see how I didn't exaggerate there?) have also commented, "She'll be a CEO someday."

Personally, I don't think that's a compliment, but it looks like she'll make more money than a writer does.

My son is a third grader, and he says approximately one word to her four, and most of those he gets out while she's at sleep-away camp.

I never know whether to tell people I'm self-employed or unemployed. It's a fuzzy line for a novelist. When I worked for magazines, I didn't feel sheepish when I called myself a writer. But now, when a book only comes out every few years–because there were television pilots and pitches that never came to fruition, drafts that were shelved, you name it–I feel like I'm flat out lying.

"Schedule" and "routine" are two things I aspire to. Here's what I *tell* myself is my schedule:

I do, in fact, always get dressed, brush my teeth and 90% of the time make the bed (which just involves pulling the comforter up and over; no fancy pillows, you understand) immediately upon waking, all of which makes me feel ahead of the game. That advantage is lost pretty quickly around the time I'm making lunches and cursing like a general running a failed military maneuver, which is what every school morning feels like. My husband and I play zone defense in the morning–one of us covers the bedrooms (up, dressed); the other covered kitchen activities (breakfast, lunch). The kids get off to school; the husband goes off to that nice job that keeps us in health insurance (thank you, honey), and when I'm deep in a book and on a roll, I do pack up my laptop and head right out to the café or library and dive in.

But it's only every few years that I'm on a roll, mind you, so other times, I bullshit around the house, doing things that absolutely need doing, but that if I do too much of them, feels like I've eaten a bag of candy--felt great while I was eating it, but now I just feel kind of sick and unfulfilled. So, every single solitary day I try to get up and out and leave dishes unwashed, Nerf bullets and sparkly things underfoot (Nerf bullets at least much less painful to step on than Legos were), and get the hell out, and I'm always, always happy when I do.

I turn on freedom as soon as I can, and if I don't, my writing suffers. I really believe that my mind fragments if I start the day with chores--whether out in the world, online, or in the house. A different set of neurons fire. That gives me an adrenaline rush, and it's hard to get back to the sedate, even soporific work of eking out a tale.

I rarely do weekends and I'm teary with exhaustion after 8pm, so I'm not one of those admirable sorts who squeezes in the writing around other responsibilities. I'm a 9-5er. Or really, on a great day, an 8:30-1:00-er. And with all this available to me, I feel as though I spend as much time doing scheduling acrobatics to afford me time to write as I do writing.

What's awesome about writing/parenting is that it's easier to do 100 things than 5, so while having the kids keeping us busier than I thought a person could be, it makes me way more efficient. After I squeezed in entire books between dealing with kids, I wondered why I hadn't squeezed out an entire series before kids.

So, being a parent has focused me. Sometimes that's an accurate statement, sometimes it's not. I will also say that ANY additional human experience makes one a better writer. So, while there are days, I wish I hadn't had kids--and there are--the more I experience, whether it's joy, tragedy, anxiety, then the more arrows I have in my quiver for pinpointing a particular emotion of a particular character. I'm even grateful for two miscarriages (I wasn't at the time) because now that's one more human experience I can relate to, examine, work into my writing.

I have an awesome work/life balance, and I know very few other women or men who can say that. It turns out I enjoy managing my household, which I think dismayed my mother at first, as she was one of the first beneficiaries of 2nd wave feminism. But if that's all I did, I think I'd become mired in minutiae. Writing satisfies me and completes me. I'm very fortunate that

I know what makes me happy and fulfilled. I don't doubt for a minute that this was what I was meant to do. And if that changes, I'll run with it."

A STORY FROM THE SALONS

Anjali Mitter Duva

Anjali mitter duva is an Indian American writer raised in France. She is the author of the bestselling historical novel *Faint Promise of Rain*, which was shortlisted for the 2016 William Saroyan International Prize for Writing and the 2015 Chaucer Award for Historical Fiction. She is also a Co-founder of Chhandika, a non-profit organization that teaches and presents India's classical storytelling *kathak* dance. Educated at Brown University and MIT, Anjali is a frequent speaker at conferences, festivals, libraries, schools and other cultural institutions.

She was a finalist for a 2018 Artist Fellowship from the Massachusetts Cultural Council. In her spare time, she runs a book club for teens and the Arlington Author Salon, a quarterly literary series. She lives in the Boston area with her husband and two daughters, and is at work on her second novel, set in 19th century Lucknow. At the time of this 2016 interview, she had just read an excerpt of her first novel at a season closing Pen Parentis Literary Salon that also featured Rick Moody. Her performance included *kathak* dance. It was spellbinding. What is also spellbinding is the incredible support system she has created with another family.

Anjali described a unique and magical way of using community to better the lives of everyone involved—no joke. This is one of the most innovative and successful ways that I have ever seen a writer manage family obligations.

"I have two daughters, ages 5 and 11. I live just outside of Boston, in a suburb that is close to the city but also has many wonderful parks, conservation land, nearby farms, a bike path and a swimming hole. Every day is different as I juggle various activities, and that's something that gives me energy. That said, I do try to focus my book writing time in the mornings while the kids are in school. But first, my family has a sit-down breakfast together, which takes some effort but is something about which we feel strongly.

My support system is something for which I am tremendously grateful. On the one hand, I have a spouse who is steadily employed, and who is unwaveringly supportive of my writing career. This is very significant, and not something I take for granted.

The second aspect of the system is the unusual and life-changing arrangement my family has created with another family. In short, my family has for the past twelve years been intertwined with another multi-cultural, two-kid family with whom we share childcare, errand-running, meal preparation, and even vacations to places near (Cape Cod) and far (Vietnam).

The arrangement began by happenstance right around when each family, living in the same building, had their first child. None of us have family around to help out (my closest relative lives in NYC, and my parents are in France) and so we created our own village. This system has been key to my being able to pursue a creative career, and it's had myriad other advantages, too, not just for me but for my husband and children.

So: once the kids are in school, I check in with my neighbor to plan out the logistics of the day. Once we've divvied up the errands, kid pickups and dinner planning, I leave the house to research and write.

Most of the time, I head to a wonderful little local café. I find the hubbub easier to block out than the quiet of the house (and its attendant chores that sit and stare at me—breakfast dishes, laundry, etc.). I've also made many friendships with other creative folk who use the café as an office. Around lunchtime, I head home and often run some errands on the way—groceries and such. I then squeeze in some time to tend to more task-oriented activities: a lot of emails, responding to interview requests, promotion tasks for my book, sending out queries for speaking gigs, that type of thing.

At 2:30, when school lets out, I turn back into Mommy (or "Maman," as my kids call me, since I speak French with them). Two days a week they are in afterschool, which gives me a bit more time. The other afternoons I spend with them, take them to French, swim, etc. Toward 5:30 pm there's a general gathering with the neighbor's kids and then dinner prep, etc.

My semi-communal arrangement with another family has been key to my sanity and my career as I juggle those with my role as a parent. My work-life balance benefits from the fact that I've been able to link all my activities to my writing, my family, and my interests. They're all interconnected.

Watching my daughters grow into little (and not so little) people, I'm grateful for the flexible schedule that allows me to spend time with them, but I'm also grateful to be able to model for them an occupation that oftentimes feels in direct contrast to the technology-driven culture of instant gratification, busywork and superficial thought that surrounds us.

My children are witnessing me spending years on a project. They are learning to respect the time and intellectual effort it takes to produce creative work. They can actually see me at work, attend my events, and eventually read my books. It's a way to share my career with them that is very gratifying. And it doesn't hurt that they both love books.

In the beginning, it felt as though parenting and writing were two separate worlds. I had to close the door to one to walk through the door to the other. Now, the gap between the two is narrowing. For one thing, I'm able to explain my activities to my children in a way that makes sense to them. I can say "I'm just finishing the outline of this chapter and then we can read a book together." They get it. Similarly, it's been easier for me to go out in the evenings to read or speak (and dance!) at events because they understand why Maman is going out as part of her work, and that these events are important to me. And they both express a sense of pride that I'm an author which is just lovely. I'm looking forward to the time, only 3-4 years away, when my books will be age appropriate for my eldest daughter to read. Perhaps it will be a pick for her book club.

One thing that helped, although I did not plan it this way, was to have my children six years apart. Even as a new mother, I felt I could hang on to my projects, work on them here and there even as my baby napped or spent a few hours with a sitter. I never felt so sucked into parenthood that I had to let go of myself, as it were. And by the time the second child came along, the first one was six, and in school, and generally able to be of some assistance, or at least to not make huge demands of me.

Nonetheless, I've had to learn to switch gears instantly, to close my computer mid-thought at 2:25 pm and listen fully to my children's chatter about school at 2:30, then go back to that thought at 9 am the next day. I've also learned to be patient. I can't do it all at once, so my first book took 10 years to write and publish, and I had to drop out of teaching dance because of the time requirements, and I can't attend most of the cultural events I'd like (who can?!), and I just don't have much downtime, but I've had to accept these facts.

I dream of some kind of subsidized, accessible program, preferably in a beautiful natural setting, to which writing parents could go with their children during school vacations. There would be little writing studios where the parents would work while the children enjoyed camp-like activities run by counselors. Meals would be taken all together, and evenings would include a variety of literary programs (workshops, readings) and family events. A retreat for everyone. Wouldn't that be nice?

I definitely struggle with not having long chunks of uninterrupted time. Having to work in short bursts of 2-3 hours makes it hard to get to—and stay in—that place where creativity really gets going. I also find it challenging to be as involved in the literary community as I'd like, given that most events, understandably, take place right around dinnertime on weekday evenings, right when it is nearly impossible for me to leave the house.

Finally, being the spouse with the "flexible" schedule means that I absorb all changes (planned and unplanned) to the schedules of the rest of my family: if a child is sick, I'm the one to stay home with her. If my husband is stuck late at work, I'm the one to cover all parenting duties, or to scramble together childcare coverage if I've got a commitment of my own. It becomes difficult to plan my writing time when so much is out of my control. Birthday parties, play dates, dentist/doctor/orthodontist appointments, swim classes, materials for school projects, grocery lists, new shoes/clothes, volunteering at school, summer camp research and sign up, all these things are constantly going swirling through my mind in the background, and shutting off that incessant chatter in order to plunge into my creative work is a serious challenge.

I don't think one can ever really be prepared for parenthood—the demands on one's time, body, emotions, but also the visceral joys of holding a little hand down the street, of feeling a warm, trusting body succumb to sleep on one's lap. What I really wish I'd known ahead of time pertains to the writing world and just how all-consuming the double job of book writer/promoter is. I hadn't anticipated that second part, the one in which the writer has to do so much work, especially as a debut author, to promote her writing and reach her audience. I thought it was difficult to juggle writing and parenthood as I wrote my first book, but little did I know it would become so much more of a challenge once my book was en route to publication!

My biggest piece of advice is to create a support network for yourself right in your neighborhood. Cultivate a very local community of like-minded folks. Be generous in helping others. Accept help yourself. Share tasks. Pool resources. Raise your children with the gift of community. Everyone will benefit."

WRITING WITH A BIG KID

Energy

With tweens you'll have energy—so long as you manage to escape the natural parental anxiety that will build every time, they have an interpersonal drama. There is a *lot* of drama to avoid. Tweens can make you emotionally drained with their declarations that no one likes them or that so-and-so's going to Greece in a private jet and why don't you have a private jet? It can be exhausting to try to pull a fourteen-year-old boy away from his absolutely most awesome Australian friends who are just sitting down to play this best-game-ever at 11am their time, which happens to be bedtime in your time zone. You'll spend an awful lot of your energy on fashion questions, on popularity issues, on bullying, on how much they hate homework. They have fierce opinions now, these pre-teens and young teens. But when they are busy, they are utterly, completely absorbed. They are finding themselves, discovering their passions. The sooner they figure out what they love, the more time you will have to yourself.

During this time period, you are mostly a taxi service—getting them to and from their activities, but they no longer want you to watch the game or to mingle with their friends once they arrive to their destination. Write in the car (again, our Pen Parentis app is hopefully going to allow you to do that!) or on the subway.

Of note is that for parents of special-needs kids, this is actually a time of even less energy and time for writing. Once kids are hitting puberty, the boys are sometimes bigger than you and the girls are definitely hormonal. Middle schools often push back on special needs services in a way that elementary schools don't. (Elementary schools will often merely delay... ask you for more tests, tell you to wait and see. Things come to a head in middle school when parents realize they better figure this stuff out before high school hits.)

That said, Marie Myung-Ok Lee and her husband are both successful writers and professors of writing. Their son (who is 20 at the writing of this book) still lives at home. J has autoimmune disease, autism and an intellectual disability. Here is a taste of how Marie fought through a crisis to finish an essay. She is a hero in my eyes - someone who has fully accepted the responsibilities that life has given her, has embraced the added burdens of her particular situation with love (and lots of Buddhism) and here is what she said about trying to finish an essay:

Early on in the COVID-19 pandemic, our son started vomiting and ran a fever. His pediatrician had just left the state and it was a panic time for all. I also had an essay due the next day—about the pandemic. I also found out from my cousin that her whole family was sick with Coronavirus (she's a nurse) and her husband was in critical condition and on a ventilator.

I had a half draft of the essay done, but in the new circumstances, it just seemed flat. It also suddenly seemed unlikely I could get it in on time (print deadlines don't wait).

However, both as a parent and a writer, I am very goal oriented. I emailed a nurse in our son's ex-doctor's office, because I was pretty sure she'd still respond, and she did. Early in the pandemic the hospitals in New York City were overwhelmed and I needed to know what to do if we indeed needed to go. She helped me put together a plan for when and what we would do if J's symptoms got worse. I know a lot about my son's health issues and started on some therapies to help him feel better. I spent the rest of the day going into his room (fully gloved and masked) taking his temperature regularly, keeping him hydrated, and also trying to induce a sweat (an old Korean remedy). He started sweating that night and his fever went down.

My essay seemed like a thing of the past, now that many of the theoretical things I feared—having the virus in the house, having someone gravely ill— seemed to be happening. Given the small amount of time I had to work on the piece while my husband watched J, I made a strange decision that, instead of finishing what I had, to start over. Starting from my new, heightened mood made everything seem like it was going a million miles an hour. I had huge, grandiose ideas, and for a change I didn't tell myself to tone it down.

Sometimes, all you can do is just get it done. I was lucky I had another place to go, away from my family, for an hour or two, to be physically away.

My editor was amazed I got it in on time, and frankly, I was, too. I think, sometimes, when it seems all too much, when you think how you can possibly get it done, that's when you really have to. If writing is really going to be part of your life, it's in all parts, and there's no need for an "excuse" to shrink away from it. Urgency in life can translate to urgency in writing.

WRITING WITH A BIG KID

Money

There is still plenty of time before college, but you should probably have a plan by now for saving for college if you plan to send your kids to school. You should also be planning for retirement. Aging parents. All the grown-up things. See the chapter on "Little Kids: Money" for a list of ways to make some extra money when you are between your own books.

Be aware: writers are rarely wealthy.

The average author with a first-time book deal from a traditional publisher can expect to receive an advance of $5,000 to $15,000. Note that this is your entire pay and that this is literally an advance on royalties. After the book is released: you won't see another dime until you have earned back that entire advance–at about $1.25 per book sold—until the advance is paid back in full. Then you will be paid by check twice annually. (Numbers from AuthorityPublishing.com)

Most contracts with traditional publishers allow the author to receive an advance (see above) and then 10% royalties on net profit from each book. If your book retails at $25 per copy, you would need to sell a minimum of 4,000 copies to break even on a $5,000 advance. (Now look at your social media to guess how many people will definitely buy your book. How many friends/families do you have that you can count on for those first sales?)

And that is just for a $25 hardcover. If your book is a 375-page novel, a reasonable to price is $16.95. Most trade paperbacks fall into the $13.95 to $17.95 price range. (Statistics from Chron.com and Mill City Press.)

But what if you nail it and your book is a bestseller? Can you expect to send Junior to Harvard? Given the royalties of a standard contract, an author selling 20,000 books priced at $25 would earn $65,625 the first week on the *New York Times* best-seller list. This is not quite the millions superstar authors bank, but if the book continues to sell, these earnings add up to an impressive income. (Numbers from Careertrend.com)

Here is a fantastic chart, downloadable online from Publishing Perspectives.com - to help you see visually what various authors earn on average in a year.

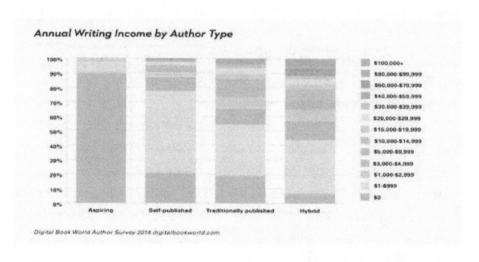

LINK:**https://publishingperspectives.com/wp-content/uploads/2014/01/dbwslide.png**

To make money writing you actually have to send out your stuff. Yes. Into the actual world.

Sell your book!
Sell your stories!
Sell essays, poems, win writing contests!

If you write genre, you are more likely to make a reasonable income than if you write literary fiction - so if you need money, you might consider commercial fiction if money is a goal for you.

Fiction writers of the literary sort tend to make their money by teaching. Their goal is generally to gain a tenured position teaching writing at a university and then spend their summers and sabbaticals writing.

No judgements here—that's just the way things are.

Ghost-writing is also an option. $20-60K per book—it's not a bad deal, and in some cases, you could get your name on the cover (if you want to).

Try to get an agent if you are trying to make money with your writing. If you write in a genre that people already voraciously buy (for example: vampire romance novels) then absolutely self-publish. Indie Publishing has no downside unless no one can find your book. But if your title turns up when people do an internet search (mysteries with downtrodden detectives) then you absolutely should consider self-publishing. You'll make a lot more money, and you won't have to worry about your book being out of print.

I recognize that not all of you already know if you want or need an agent—there is a section in the back talking about how to get an agent, if that is where your desires lie, but there are many blogs and articles already written about that topic. The publishing industry has shifted so drastically and is under such duress, that everything I tell you might be different in the next 24 hours.

If you have already decided whether to go with a traditional publisher or to be an indie publisher you are on track, if not, there are lots of services that can help you make this choice. Oh, and yes, "self-publishing" has been beautifully and successfully rebranded as "indie publishing" which sounds just as good as "traditional publishing"—which it actually IS if you and your book are suited to it.

A STORY FROM THE SALONS

Stewart Lewis

Stewart lewis is a seven-time published author and singer-songwriter who is based out of Nashville, TN and Nantucket, MA. His novels have been translated into five languages and his songs have been used in TV and film worldwide. His latest novel, Happily Whatever After, called "Charming" by 1 New York Times Bestseller Elin Hilderbrand, will be published in July 2020.

He read twice at Pen Parentis, once commuting up from Washington, DC where he and his husband relocated from New York City. At the time of this interview, his daughter was eight. (Her name has been edited from the interview to respect her privacy).

"Setting goals, like selling a book every year, helps me achieve work-life balance. I call it, *staying on the bus.* I feel better as a person when I am accomplishing work. I have the support of my husband, and [my daughter] has occasional playdates and does horseback riding and trapeze school to allow me to have time to write.

My daughter recently saw that a mother of one of her friends was reading one of my books. I was instantly "cooler" in her eyes. That was rewarding. It's also just nice to feel a close connection with a person who is part of you, to experience that love, which finds its way into characters and situations in my work.

More than anything, I want [her] to read books, and not spend her whole formative years staring at a screen. She has gotten into a fantasy series and is on the fourth book. While it's not the genre I write, I am thrilled that she is reading. I told her it will make her smarter. She doesn't like to listen to dad much, but I think she deeply respects that I am a writer, and she even writes herself sometimes.

Draw boundaries, and make sure you have time to write. Don't beat yourself up about it. Kids need to learn to have their own time as well. It has taught me a lot of patience. If anything, I want to work harder and be more successful to set a good example for her, and to be able to provide for her. And one day, hopefully, she'll read one of my books, and we'll sit down and talk about it. I can't wait for that conversation!"

THE BIG KID YEARS

A *Summary*

During the big kid years (late elementary and middle school), most writers find a groove as regards time and energy to writing. Second, third and fourth kids are frequently still in younger stages though, and in writing as all careers, it is the youngest kid's needs that will most affect your ability to get work done (unless you have a special needs kid in which case, that distinction will be forever theirs).

In the big-kid years, money will likely start to become more of a motivator, as many writer-parents stop writing and take on lucrative or at least more reliable forms of income. To keep your creative writing muscles strong during this time, particularly if you have had to take on an extra job or two to pay the bills, make sure to set weekly goals that flex those muscles. Enroll in a class for some outside stimulus, join one of our accountability groups, or just do a series of creativity exercises from any online source.

Here are some phrases to google that will give you lots of choices:

1) *quick creativity boosters*
2) *creativity exercises for writers*

3) *story starter generator*

And if you prefer more "yoga-type" language:

4) *unblock your creativity*

Remember that once you have an idea it helps to actually run with it. Try to finish what you start, even if you can only work on it in short bursts.

Also— during this time in your kid's life, try to send out your work. If you want to be paid, consider using a website like the Submission Grinder (**thegrinder.diabolicalplots.com**) which is free but leans toward genre publications, or Submittable (**submittable.com**) which is also free but posts mostly literary-journals and contests. Contests can also be found on Poets & Writers free website (**pw.org**). Be aware that contests frequently ask for submission fees because their income is used to support the working of nonprofit publications. Finally, there are services that you can pay to send out your manuscripts, of which **duotrope.com** is the most well-known.

As far as I can tell, the efficacy of any submission tracker in getting paid for your work is greatly connected to the enthusiasm of the user paired with the marketability of whatever they are writing.

In other words: write it first, sell it later.

A short word about multiples:

Okay people, deep breath.

The amount of parents having just one child seems to be fluctuating as quickly as the world is changing. Each kid will exponentially affect your time, energy and money (though according to people with truly large families, at some point, they become more a help than hindrance!) and additionally there is no way to know if your only child will be one that requires every bit of your time and energy or if everything will run smoothly until you add the fifth.

Obviously, twins are harder (but Darin Strauss won the National Book Critics Circle Award while his twins were young) and having larger families will require more parenting time (but Laura Vanderkam managed to publish six nonfiction books so far and she has four kids—notably, she writes and speaks about time management for professionals).

The point here is that yes, of course, it is much much harder to find time for any activity that requires focus with two or more children pulling that focus away. There is not much you can do about that.

The best advice I have heard is to take a set period of time — three months to a year — and just explore various ways you write and see what feels second best, because the optimal "everything is quiet and I'm devoted to my work for hours at a stretch" doesn't exist anymore. Writing your second-best way will require adjustment, so instead of working on one longer piece, you can do prompts (many blogs and websites offer writing prompts for free), try short form poetry or flash, or write very short essays.

Recognize that just as your kids will have to adjust to each others' sleeping patterns and eating habits (and allergies and other special needs), so will your career. Even the best writerly setups will likely change as each kid grows into the next stage, particularly if you are sharing your work space with anyone else in the family.

Most important: forgive yourself for accomplishing less than before, but don't walk away from the whole career. Children DO grow up—and when they do, you want to be ready to jump into a longed-for project. Do research, write in microbursts, join an accountability group or partner up with another parent writer to exchange short pieces.

Also remember that putting kids to work builds their character. Assign quiet book-time to the whole crew. If you can afford it, join a writing space once per week for a few hours (or just sit alone in your parked car and write there!). Have your oldest try their hand at making breakfast or dinner for the younger. Nothing has to be perfect, you just need to find a way to give yourself about twenty minutes every few days. Novels have been written that way - but more importantly, high quality shorts have been written and published and in this way, careers have been saved. Break your projects down into small tasks, do your best, and find community with people who will celebrate your wins.

PART 6

Writing with A Teen

WRITING WITH A TEEN

Time

The beauty of writing with a teenaged child in the house is that you truly have almost all the time you had before you had kids. You rarely see teenagers; they follow their own schedules; they are usually holed up in their bedrooms or not in the house at all. By the time they are sixteen they have learned to drive or have discovered public transportation, and their activities keep them so busy they often don't even show up for dinner (or at least, many don't!). The older the teen, the less of your time they will physically need. Even parent-teacher conferences are few and far between, and in high school these last under half an hour. Your child is no longer an excuse for taking up your time—so if you haven't already set up a new writing schedule by middle school, definitely now is the moment to begin.

Setting up your new writing schedule and having a project is actually an urgent matter during the four years of high school because when your kid leaves home to go to college or gets a job and moves out, you will suddenly be faced with an empty home and no idea how to begin to write. Start your new routine now, while you still have occasional distractions! Come up with a project, even if it is just to collect and look at the stories you wrote over the last fourteen years to see if there is enough for a collection.

You will have the time for this.

Isn't that glorious news? You get your time back.

Do some spiritual exploring: do you prefer to write in the mornings? Afternoons? Late at night? Your teen will probably offer you the opportunity to do any or all three. I found that when my son turned sixteen and started staying out late, the only way for me to stay sane was to bury myself in creative writing — otherwise I would fret and worry and wonder where he was and how he was doing. Writing was the perfect distraction. And this was when I first started writing in the horror genre can't possibly have anything to do with the fact that I was writing while my son was out....!)

Give yourself goals and deadlines. If you do not yet have a writing community, this is the perfect time to find out who in your area is a writer. Some ways to find writing communities are:

1) Take a writing class, either standalone or a Continuing Ed in a local college or university. The other students you meet often are the best source for a writing community. You might even find beta-readers (aka "first readers") who you can trust with early drafts of your manuscripts.

2) Join a writing workshop—they are often posted on flyers in coffee shops or libraries, or sometimes if you join a book club you will find that one or two of the other participants are writers. (The difference is that in a class there is an instructor teaching you writing lessons in a structured way, and usually the edits you get are kept between you and the instructor, whereas in a workshop you and your peers exchange work and discuss the edits in a public way, often moderated by a "leader.")

3) Look online - meetup.com is a great place to meet other writers, Facebook has first-readers groups and writing groups. Pen Parentis has a community online on Facebook (facebook.com/penparentis then search for "Pen Parentis Behind Closed Doors" — it is a secret group so you have

to search it and request membership, but if you have a child and you are a writer serious about working hard, we are glad to have you!)

4) Attend readings and book signings at local bookstores. This is a slower way of becoming a part of a writing community, but when you have been noticed at one or two events, sometimes you can strike up conversations—this is particularly useful for people who write genre.

5) Also, for genre: online communities such as HWA, SFWA, PEN America, Author's Guild, RWA—also young adult, middle grade fiction, children's books, society for illustrators—these genres have very strong (though sometimes also controversial) guilds and associations. Visit them and join if you feel they are for you. They all sponsor events, and at these events you can find people that write what you write.

6) if you can afford it and if you can get away, writing residencies and art/writing colonies are a fantastic place to find other writers. They range from very hands-on lecture-based situations similar to summer camp, to isolated cabins where someone mysteriously delivers your food in a basket and leaves you alone for the whole day to write. Most of these magical places have at least one or two social events (most have far more social than isolation!) to get the writers to meet each other, and nearly all of them have alumni cocktail parties. Some very helpful places are Cave Canem, Millay, Yaddo, MacDowell, Hedgebrook.... These are exclusive and hard to get into, but once you are in, it's like having a doctorate from Yale in drama or a law degree from Harvard. You're in a club of fantastic writers who also made the cut—and club members help one another. It's how the world works.

* With kids it is notoriously hard to get away to one of these colonies, many are six to eight weeks long and what parent would find it easy to

get away from a young child for that long? Pen Parentis has been working towards raising the visibility of the unfairness of this practice for parents, given the extreme aid that residencies give to writers. At writing, Sustainable Arts Foundation is funding ten new programs per year to increase parent participation at various writing programs, residencies, and colonies. Their support includes things like shorter residency times, money for childcare, ability for small children to visit, child activities during the day—many various and creative ways to allow parents to take part and gain the networking benefits of these amazing retreats.

A STORY FROM THE SALONS

Jamie Brenner

Jamie Brenner grew up in suburban Philadelphia on a steady diet of Norma Klein, Judy Blume, and Judith Krantz novels. After studying literature at The George Washington University in Washington, D.C., Jamie moved to New York City where she started her career at HarperCollins Publishers, then later Barnes&Noble.com and Vogue.com before returning to books and becoming an author. Her novel *The Forever Summer* was a national bestseller. People Magazine says of her latest novel, *Drawing Home*, "the pages practically turn themselves."

Jamie read for Pen Parentis in February 2018. Her daughters, both teenagers, inspired this online interview we conducted shortly thereafter.

I write every day, usually from around 9 to 3. I try to compartmentalize — I get my writing done first, then deal with appointments and errands for the kids. We live in New York City, so they can get around by themselves (I don't have to drive them anywhere.) But any doctor appointments, parent-teacher conferences, shopping excursions, etc. I try to do only after the writing day is finished. Can't always accomplish that! On weekends, I try to be more available, but depending on what stage of the book I'm at, I sometimes have to keep to the 9–3PM schedule. But if I've been busy, I try to take Sunday afternoons off to walk around downtown or see a movie with one or both of my daughters if they want. (I recently saw *Ladybird* with my oldest.) I find its most important to be available at night, to talk to them about their day and troubleshoot anything that might be going on. Also, to make sure they're doing their homework. The tricky time of year is the spring and summer when I'm on a book tour and away some time.

I love that I can set an example for my daughters that it's possible to do what you love and make a living. They see that I work hard, that I have taken risks. I know that they are proud of me. My oldest is also a writer and has won awards for her poetry and short fiction. I don't know if that is nature or nurture, but it makes me very happy! My husband (second husband, not the father of my children) is very supportive. He will jump in to get day-to-day things done or take the girls to an appointment if I am on deadline or travelling. He completely respects what I do, and it's a priority for him. I don't know if I have work-life balance. I have definitely heard from my daughters, "You work all the time!" But again, I think I am setting an example of working hard to achieve a dream.

The challenge of being a writing parent has changed as my children have grown. Teenagers notice that you're distracted—they can take it personally. In terms of technical time, it was more difficult when they were very young. I remember having babies at home and struggling to get writing in during naps. I will take teenagers over babies any day!

Advice? Take your writing seriously—don't let anyone make you feel it is a hobby or that you are being indulgent. You don't need permission—remember that.

WRITING WITH A TEEN

Energy

So, yay! You have a teenager, and suddenly you have all the time in the world. Here's the downside: you have a teenager. You have a creative imagination. There is no moment of any day at which you will not be worried. When they are home, you'll wonder if they are doing their homework like they told you they would. When they are out, you'll wonder if they are with the people you think they are with. You'll wonder what they are doing. You'll wonder where they will go for college, if they can get in, if they even want to finish school. You'll wonder and worry, and your excellent creative imagination will be exhausted by the time you sit down to write fiction. So even though they aren't physically taking your time, the worry will exhaust you, and your energy levels will be quite possibly lower than they were when you had a newborn. It's like this crazy cycle—but don't worry, people get through it. They do. And you will, too.

They won't be teenagers forever.

One thing that parents of teenagers have told us they didn't expect was the mental paradox of wanting to write like they did before they had kids but suddenly seeing their writing through the eyes of their child. What will my teenager think of this sex scene? What lesson am I teaching kids my daughter's age? It is a weird moment of realization—but again, you can *and should* overcome this. It's no different from when you began writing and felt awkward because "what if my Great Aunt Mary reads this?" To be a writer is to write for your perfect reader. Not your teenager and not the imaginary disapproving teenager in your brain. Most of the writers who read on our stage having published difficult novels or memoirs while a teen was in the house reported that their kids never read a word of what they wrote. Even when offered. A small portion of the memoirists did say they ran the portions about their child past their child and got approval—but not many did that, mostly only the ones with significantly older children. And to make you happy: every one of the kids in these memoirs were delighted to be featured in a book.

All the writers who brought adult children to their Pen Parentis readings (we don't allow children under 21) were universally delighted by how proud their children were of their writer-parents, and how much these adult children wanted them to succeed. At our December 2010 salon, Liz Rosenberg was scheduled to read, but her young daughter had fallen ill so she stayed home. Her adult son, Eli Bosnick, appeared in her stead, and not only did he astonish us by offering to perform incredible card tricks and other tabletop magic to entertain the guests, but he read his mother's poetry in her place. His introduction of his mother's work was unforgettable—you haven't lived until you see the newly adult son of a writer give a glowing and reverent introduction explaining how dedicated his mother is to her writing and how fortunate he was to have the opportunity of growing up with such a brilliant a writer as a parent.

So, the mental issue of "how can I write this if my child will read it one day"—is all in your head. Give your child some credit. They are the child of a writer, after all, and will hopefully therefore have a very open mind, at least as it concerns creative writing!

And if not.... well.... maybe they'll write a very successful memoir one day?

WRITING WITH A TEEN

Money

I sure hope you are sitting down. Teenage years are the absolute worst, as regards your own need for money. Somehow, it coincides with either middle or older age and you have your own needs (retirement doesn't seem like such a far-fetched idea) and you probably have aging parents, which leads to more monetary consequences. So, it's a terrible time to suddenly need money.

But then here's your teen, who likely doesn't have a job that could pay their own rent yet, who likely depends on you for everything and who has suddenly blossomed into a person who cares about clothing labels, or "the right" gaming equipment, or a world-class gymnast who travels everywhere for competition, who wants to redo their babylike bedroom, or needs a fourth tattoo, or develops a drug habit, bulimia, or anxiety from being too perfect, or gets pregnant, or wins a partial scholarship to Middlebury College and has begged you to cough up the rest of the annual $50K for four years.

Oh heavens. Let's table the discussion of college. Hopefully, you were responsible (I wasn't) and set up a great savings plan (I didn't) and have the minimum suggested savings of $200K per child already in the bank, gathering interest at a phenomenal rate. (I know a few people who did this, and I envy them every time I skip my morning latte and put the five bucks into a sad little jar.)

But even without the gargantuan expense of college, teenage years are the time when your lovely offspring suddenly feel themselves to be adult and therefore entitled to criticize you and how you have been raising them for more than a decade. These are the years when you will be hounded for decisions like sending them to preschool ballet class ("Mom! I was two!! If you had just put that two thousand dollars in a bank, I would be able to get my tongue quadruply pierced right now, no problem!") or taking them on vacation ("Dad! We could just as easily have spent spring break here at home as in Egypt seeing the stupid pyramids. There were dozens of cool parties I missed! Do you hate me that much? The pyramids are going nowhere! These parties will never happen again!")

(Like my teenaged voice? My kids are 17 and 13 right now, so I'm really good at making fun of it.)

In any event, the guilt that you will feel, rightly or wrongly, about all the parenting decisions you ever made will culminate in these next ten years of parenthood. As your kids get older, they will develop more opinions and sadly, their intelligence will grow much quicker than their wisdom. Half of the accusations they make will entail the judgment of a teen (that a drug-heavy party might be more important to their future happiness than a trip to Giza, for example) but I promise, the self-searching as you try to give your budding adult the benefit of the doubt will absolutely affect your ability to write. Even if you are a hardcore, no-nonsense, absolutely sure-of-yourself parent, your teenager has the magic key to your vulnerabilities and will waste no time exploiting that knowledge.

They will. Even the great ones.

This is not a threat to you as a parent. I went to so many parenting seminars in order to address this, and the best advice I got was from a West Coast mom I was talking to via email while waiting for a violin lesson to end.

"Children are waves," she said. "Their job is to crash and explode and get everywhere and the more the flail the better they are at their job. A parent has to be the rock that they can crash against over and over and over. Our only job is to keep as much of our own shape as possible while being crashed against."

You get that? Our job is not to stop the wave from crashing. In fact, if we do manage to completely subdue the wave, it is no longer a wave. Who likes a beach with zero surf? That's not a beach, that's a bay.

Our job is to keep our own shape, despite the crash of the waves.

Money is one place where that is going to hurt a lot because in the USA, we measure success based on how much money we are free to spend. We just do—it's been a capitalist country from the beginning. It's not really how much money we HAVE so much as how flagrantly we are able to waste it. Isn't that crazy? But just think about it—the only way that we are able to judge another person's wealth in this country is not by knowing how much money they actually have in savings; we have zero idea about that. We can glean their job income to some extent (most of the time), the exact value of their real estate holdings (thanks Zillow), and every other thing that we know about a person's wealth comes from the observation of the objects that they own and the way in which they live. If a person buys dinner for the whole room, we assume they can afford it. If they lose their Versace luggage and this is a matter of zero importance to them, we make the same assumption. There is a basic assumption in the US that people who waste money can afford to do so.

(Side note: I think that this is becoming less true, thanks to a combination of easy credit, powerful advertisements, personalized marketing, and the peer pressure of all forms of media. I think that young people today start out expecting to take on debt for college, cars, and first homes, and the distance between that debt and crippling consumer debt is truly miniscule.)

Our teens have been raised in a culture where it truly looks like everyone buys what they desire the most and simply pay for it later. They find any resistance to this method of budgeting incomprehensible.

A writer's income is by nature unpredictable. Even if you write a nonfiction book on a subject that is timely and apt to change the world, even if that book is published traditionally and picked up by talk shows and poised to sell a million copies worldwide, even then, there's every chance that a natural disaster, or—even!—a random act of stupidity by a celebrity that piques the interest of the press, will eclipse the coverage of that book, and if it doesn't sell the appropriate numbers of copies in the "important" first week, no one will care that it was because Tokyo was attacked by actual aliens. That book is toast.

Some numbers just for kicks: to be put on the bestseller list in the *Wall Street Journal*, you have to sell about 3,000 copies in your first week—and if you are looking for a spot in the *New York Times* on that same list, you'll need to sell more than 9,000—in the first week. This is why your published or nearly published author-friends are so desperate to have you "like" their author pages on Facebook, and to follow them on Twitter even if you hate Twitter. They are hoping that every acquaintance will either pre-order a book or spread the word to other communities that might pre-order a book—all to boost their first-week sales so that the title will land on a list that is widely enough published that legitimate fans of their topic or their genre or their writing style might have a hope of knowing that this new book is out in the world. That's why books on the LA *Times* bestseller list are rarely also on the *Boston Globe*'s bestseller list. Even the most avid readers in Boston are unlikely to read the LA *Times*' books section, so how can they know that a book that is wildly popular in California even exists? It's all about reaching potential fans. And the crazy thing is, if you are into this sort of marketing, there are dozens of How-To blogs on the internet to help you hit a bestseller list.

I have collected a few of these tricks below. I'm not recommending them per se; I'm just showing you how easy it is to find ways to game this system. If you go down this path, you will find your own gurus to follow. (Hint: most of them will ultimately charge you to buy *their* bestselling book called (you guessed it) some version of *How to Write a Bestseller*.)

Your goal should be to write your book. Finish it. Have a book manuscript.

When it's done, maybe you'll want to play this game to get better sales. Or maybe not. Let it be a choice and not something that stops you from finishing your book.

Amazon:

https://www.tckpublishing.com/how-to-become-a-1-bestselling-author-on-amazon/

NY Times and other Newspapers:

https://scribewriting.com/get-best-seller-list/

Or

https://www.entrepreneur.com/article/280520

Or

https://www.huffingtonpost.com/tucker-max/how-to-get-on-every-best-_b_11547678.html

There are books, video series, YouTube channels—many people would love to make money explaining to you how you can market your own book to bestseller status.

The most important thing to remember—and this is just as valid for those of you who desperately need money as for those who just want to know that a few copies of your book are out in the world—to sell a book you have to have written one.

Go write.

Finish your book.

A STORY FROM THE SALONS

J. P. Howard

JP Howard is nationally recognized for her long-running NYC-based poetry salon, Women Writers in Bloom. A black lesbian poet, she is both activist and nurturer to her writing community, and sole curator of her reading series. Besides her own writing, she runs writing workshops and community discussions—and is a full-time public interest attorney! Her debut poetry collection, SAY/MIRROR, was a 2016 Lambda Literary finalist.

She is also the author of *bury your love poems here*. JP was a 2019 featured author in Lambda Literary's LGBTQ Writers in Schools program. She was a Split this Rock Freedom Plow Award for Poetry & Activism finalist and is featured in the Lesbian Poet Trading Card Series from Headmistress Press. JP was the recipient of a Judith A. Markowitz Emerging Writer Award and has received fellowships and grants from Cave Canem, VONA, Lambda, Astraea and Brooklyn Arts Council (BAC).

JP is an Editor-at-Large at Mom Egg Review online and Co-edited *Sinister Wisdom Journal Black Lesbians—We Are the Revolution!* Her poetry is widely anthologized. JP holds a BA from Barnard College, an MFA in

Creative Writing from The City College of New York, and a JD from Brooklyn Law School.

She read at Pen Parentis in January 2019, and at the time of this interview, her younger son was fourteen and had just started high school.

"My schedule is busy! I work full time as a public interest attorney and some days I can deal with as many as 70 or 80 litigants in the courthouse where I work. My workday usually flies by because I'm so busy. I'm married, and my wife and I recently celebrated 25 years as life partners and lovers, which was pretty sweet. Together we Co-parent our youngest son, who is 14 and just started high school this past fall. Our oldest old son goes to college. I usually come home and make dinner for my family after work, then chill for a while with my wife, before I work on my own poetry, prepare for my poetry workshops, give feedback to poetry students enrolled in my workshops and/or work on promoting and scheduling my monthly literary salons later in the evening.

Usually my most productive, creative writing time is when everyone else in our home is asleep! Late nights and weekends are when I get my best writing done, but unfortunately, not always on a consistent basis. I definitely struggle to balance my time between attorney work, creative writing work, parenting and being a supportive spouse/partner. It's a balancing act, and probably my biggest challenge is carving out enough time to center and focus on my creative writing. I'm currently working on editing one new full-length manuscript and one chapbook-length manuscript. I also am working sporadically on a memoir-in-progress that has a long way to go!

I have a group of poet friends who often give me feedback and encourage me to center my writing priorities or listen when I vent about not meeting writing goals. They always encourage me to continue with those goals. I also have a group of poet friends who I have been participating in National Poetry Month (NaPoMo) exchanges (online) with for over eight years, possibly longer. Every April we exchange a poem a day and the last few years I've committed to being a part of two separate NaPoMo groups, which is one of my most productive writing months, thanks to my brilliant community of poet friends.

Writer friends/writing communities help to get me back into a frame of mind to be creative. They provide a safe space for me to share both my literary disappointments and successes.

Now that my children are older and basically self-sufficient, I have the ability to devote more time to my writing without having to worry about childcare, etc. My youngest son is a teen now, so we don't collaborate as much on our poetry together as we used to, but a highlight of parenting with a child poet was our many poetry collaborations when he was younger.

Make sure to carve out writing/solo time and set those schedules up early on, when possible, to get your writing done. Establish that writing schedule/solo time early on with your partner if you are Co-parenting. Don't be too hard on yourself. Even a half hour of solo writing time is an accomplishment, especially when balancing writing while parenting."

A STORY FROM THE SALONS

Adam Penna

Adam Penna is a poet and the author of *Talk of Happiness, Small Fires, Little Flames, Little Songs & Lyrics to Genji,* and *The Love of a Sleeper.* His work has appeared in many literary magazines and journals, including *Cimarron Review, Nimrod* and *Verse Daily.* He has been twice nominated for a Pushcart Prize. Penna is a professor of English at Suffolk County Community College and lives in East Moriches with his wife and family.

This interview was conducted in 2015, only a short while after he moved in with his then-fiancée and her two young teen children.

"I was giving a reading about a year and a half ago and a man in the audience asked me what I do when I'm writing a poem, looking for the right word, and my stepdaughter interrupts. I had to explain that, for me, who was childless so long, I welcome the interruption. I can still remember when there were no interruptions to confront. I've got notebooks, hundreds of pages, thousands of drafts of poems, which I would've traded to be interrupted like that just once back then. My colleague and friend once told me that given the choice between writing a poem no one was likely to publish and holding his daughter, well, there was no choice. You put the poem down.

But there's another story, perhaps apocryphal, about William Faulkner I like to tell when teaching him to undergrads. It's the one about his daughter's birthday. She wakes to find her father nursing an incredible hangover and asks him, "Please, Daddy, don't drink today." Faulkner replies, "No one remembers Shakespeare's daughter." I don't know if this ever happened, but I know there is this understanding that one can't be an artist and a parent. The implication is on every page of Woolf's *A Room of One's Own*, and even Jesus says, "Sell everything you own and follow me."

Writers aren't saints, though, and I think this choice between family and art is as false as the choice laid before us in grad school, when we're asked to choose poetry or prose. I've had this longstanding debate with my office mate about the role family and parenting plays in our writing lives. When I was still without children, I had the luxury to write all day, every day, and for many of those days, I did just that. But I'm with the poet who says the problem with being a poet is figuring out what to do with the other 23 hours of the day. The crisis of retiring amounts to figuring out that all you didn't have time to do when you were working and raising a family can be accomplished in about a month. So, what do you do with the rest of your time? Obviously, I write fewer poems and fewer pages now that I've got a family. It's all fairly new to me. I haven't yet learned to balance my writing life and my professional and familial lives. I knew that this would happen going in. Still, I was all in. Now that I've gotten used to the requirements of being a stepdad, I can return to the page. This means searching out the solitude for thinking and writing.

The kids are both school age. This means there are hours of the day when the house is quiet, and no one is home. I live with another writer so there is mutual respect and understating. She and I must, therefore, guard, as Rilke says, each other's solitude. This seems to me to be essential not only to love but art. What better gift can a family give than the guarantee that what they hold sacred will be treated so?

The proper perspective means knowing what is and isn't important. Humility means knowing your limitations. I can't say I've mastered either of these concepts, but I know both are required for parenting and writing. And yet both writing and parenting require us to go beyond ourselves, too. There are days when I feel like I don't have any more to give. There are days when nothing is greater than my love. I've talked about the support I receive above, and balance in this case means proper perspective. I've known, as a poet, that I'm in it for the long haul. I know that all parenting, if its genuine, means being in it for the long haul. This realization is not daunting, but a relief. Maybe the reward of being a writing parent is this. You know that each complements the other. What it takes to write, it takes to love. What it takes to care, it takes to care about each word in its right place.

Maybe the main difference, then, between my old childless life and this one is getting the timing right. I've got more balls to juggle, no doubt, but that just means I have more to write about, more sources of inspiration. The last book I wrote strikes one note. My life had been consumed by one theme, childlessness. I put that down to pick up a fuller range of notes, a whole scale of them. If at first the melody sounds sour, so be it. That is the price for learning a new instrument. The lessons I learned on the old lyre aren't lost now that I'm playing a piano.

One final thing: after the reading a year and a half ago, Shannon, my fiancé, reminded me of a truer and better answer to the man's question about interruptions. My stepdaughter walked in one afternoon while I was writing a poem and asked me what I was doing. "I'm looking for a word," I said. Then she read the poem with me. "Hymn," she said. "The right word is hymn." And she was right."

THE TEEN YEARS

A *Summary*

Expect periods of increasing hormones and rages escalating into scattered conflicts. Hope for the best. Do what you can. Teens are distracting when they are around and even more distracting when they are absent. Your writing will either be a refuge, or it will be impossible.

Do your best.

Take the extra time and do what you can.

Now is the time to reconnect to yourself as a writer, to find that big project, start the novel, collect the flash or the stories or the poetry into a whole long collection and see if you can win a contest or get it published. This is you-time, even though it won't feel like it.

Go for it now, make yourself a name.

Remember who you are.

Hunker down into your writing routine.

Write.

PART 7

Writing with An Empty Nest

WRITING WITH AN EMPTY NEST

Time. Energy. Money. All of it.

Congratulations! Your child survived to adulthood and is out there doing something. Hopefully it's something that delights you. There is every chance in today's world that your fully grown-and-flown adult child will at some point come back to sleep in their old room (your new writing studio) or on the couch or the floor for a while. That's okay. It's life. It happens. Go with the flow. Remember everything you've learned about being a writer: jot down ideas whenever they come, carve out some writing time and a writing space, don't fret too much about early misses, keep sending out. Find a supportive workshop or reader's group. Everything in writing is long-term. Don't get discouraged. Even with an empty nest, it may take a while for you to get back to your pre-child writing self.

But oh, the rewards if you do!

Think back to before you had kids when the hardest thing was just sitting down to write. That's where you are again. So, get your mind off your troubles and get back in the game. Hopefully you've never left! You've got a pile of ideas you are eager to begin. Apply for a residency to Yaddo. Get a Fulbright. Accept a Fellowship to teach at Exeter as a Writer in Residence.

Your time, energy, and money are (mostly) your own.

Until you have grandchildren.

Whatever is left is all yours.

I really just want to leave this page blank.

Maybe I will.

Your kid is grown and flown and now you have a vacant room to deal with (Shrine? Gym? Air B&B? Guest room? Office?) and more time than you know how to fill.

Go write something. I'll wait.

A STORY FROM THE SALONS

Lucille Lang Day

Lucille Lang Day is the author of a memoir, Married at Fourteen: A True Story, which received a PEN Oakland Josephine Miles Literary Award and was a finalist for the Northern California Book Award in Creative Nonfiction. She has also published two children's books and ten poetry collections and chapbooks, Co-edited two poetry chapbooks and Co-authored a nonfiction textbook called How to Encourage Girls in Math and Science. Her short stories, poems, and essays have appeared widely in literary magazines and anthologies, and her many honors include the Willow Review Award for Creative Nonfiction, the Blue Light Poetry Prize, the Joseph Henry Jackson Award in Literature for her poetry collection Self-Portrait with Hand Microscope, a Notable Essay citation in Best American Essays, and ten Pushcart Prize nominations in poetry and prose. The founder and director of a small press, Scarlet Tanager Books, she also served for many years as the director of the Hall of Health, an interactive museum in Berkeley.

This interview was conducted in 2015, a few years after she read at our annual Winter Poetry Salon.

"I have always lived in the San Francisco Bay Area. My first daughter was born when I was 15, my second when I was 26, and much of the time, I was a single mother. For about 30 years I had to balance school, jobs, motherhood, and writing. During that time, I finished high school and college, earned an MA in zoology and a PhD in science/mathematics education, and held various jobs, including math/science specialist in a public-school district, community college instructor, technical writer, and science writer/editor at a national laboratory. After my daughters were grown, I earned an MA in English and an MFA in creative writing and worked for 17 years as director of the Hall of Health, an interactive museum in Berkeley, before finally being able to work full-time at my creative writing.

My younger daughter, Tamarind, is now 40. My older daughter, Liana, would be 51, but she died of non-Hodgkin's lymphoma in 2013. Each of them had two children, a boy and a girl who now range in age from 4 to 12. As the grandmother of four, I baby-sit often, and the new millennium has brought me a cornucopia of new opportunities to balance writing time with time spent caring for children.

When my daughters were small, I wrote primarily at night after they went to bed or while they were at school if I had the day off from work or my own classes. Sometimes I wrote until 1:00 or 2:00 in the morning. As my daughters got older and I started working full time, I got into a routine of writing on weekends and holidays. I found I was more alert and productive working in the morning than I had been during the years of writing at night. Now I'm in the habit of answering email in the morning and writing in the afternoon. It would probably be better to do it the other way around, but I'm always curious to check my email and usually end up doing that first. I don't write every day, and I find that I spend as much time on the business of writing—such as submissions, interviews, readings, and social media—as I do on my creative work.

Advice to new parents who write. Think about support systems from the beginning, as part of your overall family-planning process. Will your spouse or partner help equally in caring for the children? Do you have a parent, sibling, or close friend who can help? How much can you afford for child-care? It's best to start asking yourself these questions and talking to others about how they envision their involvement as soon as you start thinking about having a child, but some of us don't get around to these questions until we already have one or more children. If that is your situation, don't be afraid to reach out to your friends and family or to take advantage of whatever resources to help busy parents are available in your community.

Also, think about how your day job will complement, support, or inter-fere with your writing. Most writers need to do something besides write to pay the mortgage and put food on the table with regularity. Many writers find it rewarding to teach creative writing or work for a literary press or organization. I found that technical writing and science writing interfered with my creative writing: whatever mental energy I had for writing got used up at work. In my free time, I found myself thinking about edits I wanted to make in the manuals I was writing or additional questions to ask the scientists I was interviewing instead of about dialogue for my short stories or images for my poems.

For me, teaching of any kind took the most time away from both my family and my writing; planning courses, teaching them, and correcting student work was a 24/7 job. A lot of people, though, are able to teach and also write. You have to figure out what works for you. I found it easiest to write when I worked as a science administrator or museum director, i.e., jobs where my primary responsibilities were neither teaching nor writing.

Most of my time with my grandchildren now takes place at night and on weekends. My third husband, Richard Michael Levine, is also a writer, and he loves taking care of the children with me. Being with them is one of the most rewarding things that we do together. Whether we're taking turns with the children or playing with them together, for both of us I think having a partner to share the responsibility augments the joy."

A STORY FROM THE SALONS

Min Jin Lee

Min Jin Lee's novel Pachinko was a finalist for the National Book Award. A New York Times bestseller, Pachinko was also a Top 10 Books of the Year for The New York Times, USA Today, BBC, and the New York Public Library. It made over 75 "Best Books of the Year" lists, including NPR, PBS, and CNN, and was one of five finalists for the One Book, One New York campaign. Apple TV owns the rights for a television serial.

Her debut novel, Free Food for Millionaires, was a Top 10 Books of the Year for The New York Times, NPR's Fresh Air and USA Today.

She read at Pen Parentis in February 2018 and captivated the audience with anecdotes of her long struggles to be published after leaving a secure job in law to try her hand at creative writing. The following is excerpted from her online interview on the Pen Parentis website:

"My only son is 20 years old. He is in college in the West Coast. I live in Harlem. When my son was younger, I had 15 hours a week of childcare, then later on, he went to school, so I wrote then.

I don't have much of a social life. I never went out when Sam lived at home.

The most rewarding thing about being a writing parent is I have great respect for time. I am always thinking about my kid. Even when he is in college. I'm pathetic. I need to get a life. To learn how to separate. To deal. I can't really offer any tips—I don't know what I'm doing. Parenting and writing changed me as my child has grown, I admit I was wrong. About most things.

I think parenting gave me far more compassion for other parents, because it's a special tribe of people who have less attention capacity than non-parents."

THE WRITER'S SNACK JAR

Extra Content for the Hungry Writer

THE WRITER'S SNACK JAR

If there's anything a writer needs to feast on regularly it's words. In this final section you'll find some words on everything from accountability and social media to how to navigate your writing career in a COVID world.

Dive into this handy resource section whenever you're in need of a little inspiration or ideas for keeping your writing life on track. After you're done, feel free to share some words of your own.

Join the Behind Closed Doors Facebook group, become a member of Pen Parentis or send me your questions, thoughts, ideas, etc. Below is the easiest way to reach me and participate in the Pen Parentis community.

THE WRITER'S SNACK JAR

A *word about The Pen Parentis Writing Fellowship for New Parents*

In 2010, I funded the first Pen Parentis Writing Fellowship for New Parents from my own pocket hoping that reading fees would cover the expense but knowing nothing for sure. I was thrilled to see a hundred entries. The nonprofit did not even exist yet, just a reading series featuring parents called The Pen Parentis After-Work Reading Series. All I wanted to do with the Fellowship was to spread the word that writers who had kids were valid. I had put up a website for the reading series and had this vague sort of idea that everyone who read would become good friends, get together and talk about writing and their kids and how hard it was to get the work done, but also how rewarding it was when something did get written or published.

That never happened. During the readings the guests would cry, the hosts would cry, we would talk about how we were going to stay in touch and never forget this moment...but at the end of the end, it was just another reading series in a city that had hundreds of them.

The curator and I would have lunch and fantasize about creating a community, but the truth of the matter was that I was trying to build a community out of people who were used to talking about writing with people who either didn't have kids of their own, or (as we aged up) who carefully avoided discussion of their children in writing circles. We were used to avoiding the topic of kids. Mentioning our kids led to conversations about kids—which led to conversations about schools—which in New York City is a topic that never ends.

But during the readings, while the audience members were asking questions about how the writers found time to write, where they found energy and how they could afford to continue to trust that one day they might get paid for this work that could take five, ten, or more years to complete—this was where the magic was. The writers awakened, opened up. For the first time, someone was asking how they did it in a way that did not feel like it also implied "but why did you ever have children in the first place?"

The response to the first Fellowship competition showed that not only was the need for this community, national, but that the idea was a good one: many people responded to that first round of entries begging to become members of an organization that had not yet been envisioned!

The first round of entries was judged based only on writing talent—we wanted to be amazed—and instead we were staggered by the handwritten notes on the covers of some of these entries, thanking us for caring about the difficulties inherent in being a writer-parent, relating how good it was to feel seen. Many of these writers were less interested in winning, than in celebrating the fact that anyone wanted them to finish a new story at all.

"Thanks to Pen Parentis, I might actually have a community and an outlet," wrote Raina L. from California.

"Thanks for striking a match to light that fire that we new parent-writers need to generate some new work and get it out there," said Beth K. from Illinois.

"I am the mother of two special-needs children, a nine-year-old who has autism and a six-year-old who has cystic fibrosis. I was thrilled to learn about this particular competition as my wonderful children certainly make it difficult to attain my personal and professional goals, even as they inspire them." Notes like that one, from Irene R. from West Virginia, were the inspiration to turn the Fellowship into an important national outreach program for Pen Parentis.

It was a joy and delight to select the winners, who always stood head and shoulders above the other entrants. We celebrate the writers that have been chosen over the years, as well as the second and third place winners and honorable mentions. So much talent. So many great stories.

MM DeVoe introduces first Pen Parentis Writing Fellow awardee Abby Sher to featured authors Darin Strauss and Jennifer Egan during Q&A Sept 2010

Here, in the order of their wins, are the Fire Ten Pen Parentis Writing Fellows:

Abby Sher
Frank Haberle
Sarah Gerkensmeyer
John Jodzio

Jess DeCourcy Hinds
Orli Van Mourik
Elizabeth Pagel Hogan
Megan Pillow Davis
Jennifer Fliss
Anjali Vaidya

What are they doing now?

Our first fellow, ABBY SHER, had nearly given up on her career but now, ten years after her fellowship win (which she said came as a surprise and a shock) is a writer and performer whose work has appeared in various anthologies and magazines. Her writing has been in The New York Times and The Los Angeles Times. She is also the author of the young adult novel KISSING SNOWFLAKES and the brand-new YA novel Sanctuary (with Paola Mendoza.) Abby has written and performed for the Second City in Chicago and the Upright Citizen's Brigade and Magnet Theater in New York. She lives in Brooklyn with her husband and children.

FRANK HABERLE is another writer who had nearly packed it in. He said he entered the Fellowship on a whim, with a story he wrote for the occasion. He told us it was the first new story he had written in years. Now? Frank Haberle's short stories have won awards from Beautiful Losers magazine and the Sustainable Arts Foundation. They have appeared in more than 30 magazines including the Stockholm Literary Review, Baltimore Review, Inwood Indiana, Necessary Fiction, the Adirondack Review, Smokelong Quarterly, Melic Review, Wilderness House Literary Review, Cantaraville, and Hot Metal Press. A professional grant writer with nonprofit organizations, Frank is also a volunteer workshop leader for the NY Writers Coalition. He lives in Brooklyn with his wife and three children, where he is working on a vast collection of micro fiction, some of which he actually sends out.

SARAH GERKENSMEYER's short story collection, What You Are Now Enjoying, was selected by Stewart O'Nan as winner of the 2012 Autumn House Press Fiction Prize, long-listed for the Frank O'Connor International Short Story Award, and chosen as winner of Late Night Library's Debut-litzer Prize—all during or right after the year of her Fellowship. She managed her book launch and readings while caring for two little boys (one and four at the time) After winning our fellowship she was a Pushcart Prize nominee for both fiction and poetry and a finalist for the Katherine Anne Porter Prize in Short Fiction and the Italo Calvino Prize for Fabulist Fiction, Sarah has received scholarships to the Bread Loaf Writers' Conference, Ragdale, Grub Street, SAFTA's Firefly Farms, and the Vermont Studio Center (which she won shortly after being named our Fellow). She was quite nervous to accept that residency, since it would mean two weeks away from her little sons—but we encouraged her and just look what she's achieved! Her stories and poetry have appeared in several literary journals, among them, American Short Fiction, Guernica, The New Guard, The Massachusetts Review, Hayden's Ferry Review, and Hobart. Her story "Ramona" was featured in a Huffington Post piece on flash fiction and also selected by Lily Hoang for the 2014 Best of the Net Anthology. Sarah received her MFA in fiction from Cornell University and now lives and writes in her home state of Indiana, where she also won the Indiana Authors Award and became a Sustainable Arts Foundation Fellow.

JOHN JODZIO flew in from Minneapolis to accept our fellowship. He went on an extended overseas stay with his wife and then two-year-old child the year of our fellowship, writing the entire time. He also won a Minnesota State Arts grant during his fellowship year. Now he is a winner of the Loft-McKnight Fellowship and the author of the three short story collections Get In If You Want To Live, If You Lived Here You'd Already be Home and Knockout. His work has been featured in a variety of places including This American Life, McSweeney's, and One Story.

Closer to home, JESS DeCOURCY HINDS is an award-winning writer of fiction and nonfiction who lives in Queens, NY. After winning our Fellowship, she was a 2015 fiction finalist in the Barbara Deming Memorial Fund competition. Her writing has appeared in Ms. magazine, Newsweek, The New York Times, Reuters.com, Seventeen, School Library Journal and Brain, Child: The Magazine for Thinking Mothers. She works as an academic librarian and runs a series brining authors to visit with high school writers. Jess has just had a second child, and she has become an active member of our Pen Parentis Meet-ups to give herself the accountability to finish her first novel.

ORLI VAN MOURIK is a fiction writer and journalist who lives in Brooklyn with her husband and two daughters. After winning our fellowship, her work was published in Brain, Child Magazine, Joyland, The Brooklyn Rail, and Psychology Today. She teaches fiction for the Sackett Street Writers' Workshop and is the director of Sackett Online.

ELIZABETH PAGEL HOGAN is a writer from Pittsburgh, PA, with degrees in Biology and American History, who creates content for children and readers of all ages. She also writes for the educational market, for a variety of ages from PK-2 to high reading level middle schoolers. Right after winning our fellowship, she revealed that her dream was to be published in Highlights magazine. Now? Her fiction stories, non-fiction articles, activities, crafts and recipes appear in many magazines including not only Highlights for Children but also Muse, and Cricket. She has a non-fiction book published by Capstone, and three fiction books for the Heinemann Literacy Project. After winning our fellowship, she became the regional advisor for SCBWI Pennsylvania: West. She has three kids.

MEGAN PILLOW DAVIS is a graduate of the University of Iowa Writers' Workshop in fiction, and when she won our fellowship, she was also hard at work, finishing her doctorate at the University of Kentucky. Her dissertation was an examination of the American freak show and its literature. She has completed that work now, and her writing has appeared, among other places, in Electric Literature, SmokeLong Quarterly, Hobart, and Paper Darts, has been featured in Longreads, Pidgeonholes, Pithead Chapel, Brevity, and Atticus Review. She has also been twice nominated for a Pushcart Prize and for Best Small Fictions. Megan is revising her debut novel, which was a semifinalist for the YesYes Books First Fiction Open Reading Period, and she has begun work on her second book. Megan has received fellowships from the Martha's Vineyard Institute of Creative Writing, and she recently completed a residency with the Ragdale Foundation. She was also named a finalist for The Baltic Writing Residency's Kentucky Writers Fellowship. She lives in Louisville, Kentucky with her family.

JENNIFER FLISS is a New York-raised, Wisconsin-schooled, Seattle-based writer with a young daughter. She was thrilled to reconnect with old New York friends when she flew out to do her reading at Pen Parentis. She holds a B.A. from the University of Wisconsin and a certificate in Literary Fiction from the University of Washington. Since winning the fellowship, her work has been nominated for the Pushcart Prize, Best of the Net, and Best Small Fictions. Her writing has appeared in The Rumpus, PANK, The Washington Post, Necessary Fiction, The Kitchn, Gigantic Sequins, and elsewhere. Her first collection of stories was a finalist for the Black Lawrence Press Hudson Prize.

And our 2020 fellow, ANJALI VAIDYA, has the best story of all! She discovered the Pen Parentis Writing Fellowship for New Parents because her sister-in-law had been an editor in New York City. Anjali had relocated to San Diego, married and had a new baby, and was desperate to continue her writing career. Educated as a scientist, she had been reporting on environmental concerns while in India, but after the baby, she told us; it was hard for her to justify writing. The contest's small word count was just the thing: she relaunched her blog and wrote one story with our tiny word count every day for a year—never entering the competition but simply using the word count as a writing prompt. At the end of a full year of writing flash fiction, Anjali decided to go ahead and enter the best piece to our fellowship competition. And she won! It was her first professional foray into fiction, and it gave her the support to throw herself heart and mind into fiction writing. She used the fellowship prize money to bring her two-year-old daughter along on a trip to India to research and work on a novel manuscript.

We are thrilled by their level of talent and by the fierce dedication to their craft. Every one of our fellows is our pride and our joy.

And what does a Fellow spend the $1000 prize on?

Here is the actual welcome letter written by Sarah Gerkensmeyer to John Jodzio on the occasion of his fellowship win (first published on the Pen Parentis Blog in 2013):

Dear John,

Congratulations on being selected as the 2013-2014 Pen Parentis Fellow! I wish I could be there at the first salon of the season to welcome you to the family in person. This letter will have to do. I thought it would be most helpful for me to take a practical approach and let you know exactly how I have spent my $1,000 award. While I hope the following budget breakdown is helpful for you, I also apologize because this is a selfish act on my part—as these notes will help me think through some of the things I am so good at avoiding (e.g. keeping close track of expenditures for tax purposes).

$457.98	travel to promote my new book, attend residencies, etc. (including airfare, lodging, food)
$50.27	several pats-on-the-back of confidence and motivation
$29.34	an astounding sense of community
$49.58	a few late-night delirious moments of: "I am not a strange alien. I am not completely in this on my own."
$138.92	my first REAL pair of leather boots, for giving readings and talks, feeling author-y, etc.
$34.26	the reassurance that this talk of balancing parenting and writing is not taboo or strange or petty or inconsequential;
$99.99	access to a built-in audience of folks who love literature (and swanky hangout spots)
$60.88	about two dozen doses of good humor, perspective, and humility
$56.74	networking—I MET KELLY LINK
$22.05	an entire year of stellar publicity for my work
$priceless	the amazing, invigorating, bold, inventive, spectacular, kind, and imaginative work that Pen Parentis does to support the literary arts, and to invite someone like little old me into this wild, wonderful world

I hope all of that adds up correctly, John. But I'm a fiction writer, not a mathematician. And even if the figures are slightly off, I hope this budget is enough to show you how amazing the honor of being a Pen Parentis Fellow truly is. You are in for one beautiful year (and beyond). So, sharpen those pencils and wipe the smudges off the computer screen and get ready to spend big.

Best,

Sarah Gerkensmeyer

THE WRITER'S SNACK JAR

A Word about Social Media for Writers with Kids

I often get asked about Social Media and Marketing for writers with kids. Frankly? It's not that much different from social media or marketing for writers without kids, except you probably have less time to allocate keeping track of all the moving parts.

Generally, writers are asked to have an author website or blog, a Facebook page, and then some other, more interactive social media accounts. What I've found with writers who have kids, is that they often blur the lines of private and public. If you can't afford (or don't want) a professional publicist, it will be up to you to keep your book in the limelight, while your family remains in the background. Treat your personal life as you would any private information in a public venue.

The hard part is that you will probably be overtired and rushed when you first create your accounts. Make plans ahead of time for what you will and won't share with the public and put a note in your calendar to check up on yourself and your sharing every six months or so. As your kid ages into their own personhood, you'll want to give them more and more privacy. After all, it's your adoring public, not theirs.

If you can keep in mind that a writer's blog and social media feed are meant to be marketing tools for your creative writing and your personal brand, it will help you to decide what you should or should not share with the entire world. Of course, by the time this is published there will be new forms of social media, and new scandals of privacy loss and corporate data collection. Try to keep aware of the threats that face you on social media as regards data sharing.

In the interest of saving a new parent some time researching all the forms of social media, here are some simple guidelines to help you understand the current (as of 2019) best uses of the various forms of social media as marketing tools for your book.

Your author website is your isolated country house–it is very personal because the only way people will know about it is if you invite them, unless they are already your friends, or if you say or do (or write!) something that makes you a celebrity–then strangers will come to see it. Your author website should have your author name in the URL. In the best case, it will be a home for all of your writing forever. You use an author website as a home base for your current and most up-to-date bio and headshots, to list all your works in print and forthcoming, to collect your media clips in one place, to offer a way to buy all of your books, to promote your events (and keep track of them for yourself and for your taxes!) and to engage your fans–either by giving a contact form (it can connect to you directly or you can ask to connect it to your agent or publicist if you have one). Many writers blog on their sites so that their fans feel connected to them. Mentioning that you have a family on your author website helps to break the stereotype that all successful authors have no kids. You don't need to put up photos or report cards. Your author website is your professional home, your storefront. It is normal to let your coworkers know you have kids, but you don't want to be the parent who never talks of anything else!

At a recent Meetup of writer-parents, we had a long discussion about the value of author websites in today's world. Some pros were that people seeking readers for public events and people seeking panelists and experts frequently use website searches to narrow their targets down, and to see what sort of person a writer could be before contacting them for an interview. It is also valuable for the author themselves to have a running list of everything they have ever published and all the awards they have ever won. At Pen Parentis, our curators and I often reference author websites for the most up-to-date author bios. When an author then comes to me to complain that their bio is outdated, we can say we went right to the source.

If you invest in an author website, keep it current!

Some writers put up separate websites for each book. Our membership responded that when the website is for yourself as a writer and not for a book in particular, you have the option of creating a very large audience rather than one that is targeted to a specific book. As always in the arts, it is great to know your own voice and have a strong "brand" as an artist. Creating a website will help you narrow that brand—nothing like having to pick a color scheme and font to represent you as a writer to make you realize that you barely know yourself! Lay out all the short stories and books you are most excited by (yours if you have them, and those of people who you adore if you don't—their cover art and themes will help you choose what to do on your own website. It is really best to do this before your child is born—because trust me, your identity will waver afterward!!)

Best practice (from the collection of authors we have seen) seems to be to be honest about your life without spilling every secret onto the site. You can write a memoir if you really want to put it all out there—your website should hold some secrets, tease, intrigue. It should be a conversation starter (with YOU) and should draw like-minded people together. Your social media, if you do it, is where the conversation can continue. Think of your website as your shop, not your office. You can stand at the counter available if someone needs something, or you can have a mysterious shop where the owner is hard to find but the stuff is really cool, or you can have a service-oriented shop where you pour your customers tea and chat with each one as they come in. Make sure you are comfortable with the shop you create - you'll spend a lot of time with it!

Most websites will have a blog. Some authors write personal stuff to engage their fans. Some just use the blog to invite their fans to events and to thank the sponsors of the events afterward. And many new parents "are honest" on their blogs and tell their fans they are distracted by their kids, or reveal silly fun stories about their kids, or just post photos because the kids are cute. Be aware that if you take too much time on your website to talk about parenting issues rather than writing issues, you'll end up with a parenting blog—and if it isn't wildly popular (say you have sixty loyal followers who read your blog every time you post) then you've made yourself a parent-blogger for sixty people.

But let's say you get 5000 followers of your crazy hilarious way of writing about your son...you will soon careen into the land of diaper endorsements and trying out new products for money. There is good money here, or at least the potential to get lots of products. This is awesome while your kid is in diapers, but that's around three years and out for most of you, so do you really want to still be DiaperPrincessTadpole when your daughter is in middle school? Brands are meant to last and grow... make sure you choose an identity that will evolve as you do! Unless you truly want to transform your image into Professional Parent, take it easy on the parenting blog entries - keep track of how frequently you write about your child rather than something to do with your writing. Writing about your kids is the slipperiest slope to getting far, far away from finishing whatever project you were working on before Baby was born.

Websites are the easy part: social media is the true time-suck and the place where most parent writers go wonky. It's difficult not to over share about your kids online. As a parent, everything you do with your kid feels of the utmost importance – and when you're a talented writer, it's so hard not to think of every blog post as "working on my writing." For some, it becomes this, and they become professional parent-bloggers and work long hours editing their blogs to perfection. Some writing-parents make money from this, ultimately selling advertising on the site or taking on sponsorships to pay for the blogging. Think long and hard before starting down this path. Social media is plagued with scandals of data sales. Blogging about family life is not for everyone.

Nor should it be! Stay on the creative track you were on before you had a child – enjoy your children and write to your family about them. Keep scrapbooks online or off, take photos to share with your inner circle. Fans can be invited to this circle for specific reasons but always keep track of your goals in social media as a writer: you want to use your posts to focus your brand and give the public information and anecdotes that will encourage them to buy and read your next book. Unless you want to write your next book about being a parent (and some of you might!) try to keep your baby scrapbooking and your blogging separate. Even bloggers need to keep some distance between their private lives and their public persona: parent-bloggers are no different. Remember that your kid is not only a character in the blog but also a living human being who will turn thirty some day and will have things to say about how you parented them. (Don't believe me? Tell me about your mom and how she respected your privacy. Or didn't.)

For family privacy issues it is best to think of the big social media venues like this:

Facebook is your living room: you choose who to invite and what they can see while they're in your "home". Think of it like you are throwing a party in your house, you determine the guest list, and no one else can see in except by trying really hard. You will spend a good amount of time curating your list of contacts and deciding if someone is family, friend, or acquaintance; this is terrific for privacy (barring all the recent scandals of people hacking information) and it is great if you have friends and fans that follow you, but don't expect everyone to see everything you put on Facebook unless you specifically tag them in a post–and even then, some people are ignoring those invitations. The better your contact lists are organized, the more likely that the right people will see the proper posts. On Facebook, the algorithm checks to see how much interaction you do—if you click "like" or one of the other emojis or comment on someone else's post, you will get more of the same. Your friends need to interact in the same way with your posts, otherwise even if you have thousands of followers, you will show up in no one's feed. Privacy is high on Facebook (other than the usual Russian scandals and possibility of data sales) but you can't count on people seeing your posts unless you specifically tag them or message them directly. That said, an enormous number of people are on Facebook. It remains the largest social media venue with 2.2 billion users globally (**https://www. dreamgrow.com/top-15-most-popular-social-networking-sites/**)   but Instagram is catching up fast with one billion users.

Instagram is a ground floor city apartment home in which there are so many windows that pretty much all passersby can peek in if they wish to, and the nicer the apartment is, the more they will peek. Instagram is visual and relies on photos and hashtags to get more people to see the posts. Many people curate their Insta-feeds, creating an online "brand" that reflects their personality, their likes and dislikes. Using hashtags (hashtags) will bring people who search for or follow those words to your Instagram feed, even if your entire feed is private—so be careful what you post on Insta. Sometimes it can be like getting dressed in an upper floor penthouse apartment and feeling safe - not knowing that the guy on the second floor across the street has a telescope!

Others? Twitter (about 300K users worldwide) is a crowded party with everyone in the room; anyone can see anything at all times, but for the most part there's so much going on that you only pay attention to the things closest to you. What mostly happens on Twitter is people yell things into this crowded room and the other partygoers constantly tell you what just happened and comment on what you just missed, and if you're active on Twitter, you're often doing the same thing. Good to know: many editors and agents, particularly of YA, are on Twitter and there are even ways to pitch your commercial book on this platform (search pitch mad and pitch wars to see if this is for you). Speaking of professional, LinkedIn is the one true professional social media platform. And it is MASSIVE. While you should absolutely and definitely be on this social media in a professional capacity, particularly if you are at all interested in a day-job or second career of any sort, there is no reason in the world your kid-blogging should ever be on LinkedIn, unless that is your actual career and/or you are a parenting guru that intends to earn a living that way. SnapChat is the opposite end of the professional spectrum; the posts 'disappear' after a limited amount of time and as such, your involvement with this is going to be a lot more as a parent trying (and failing) to monitor your teen's posts than as a writer. Tumblr and Pinterest are losing popularity, but both are visual based micro-blogs, though Pinterest is more like a virtual bulletin board of things you want to save.

Hope that was helpful!

THE WRITER'S SNACK JAR

A Word About Accountability

You might think parenting has made you solitary—you don't really connect with the other parents; you want to talk about your writing instead of your child's feeding habits and allergies. No one gets you. That is what a writing community is all about. People who can talk to you about your goals and dreams and obstacles and who will encourage you through all of it. Pen Parentis was founded on the belief that being able to talk about your writing career with other parents who are also dealing with the same obstacles of time management, money needs, and lack of energy, will give encouragement and cause more new books to be completed by writers who happen to have kids.

The writer-parents in our Meetups have come up with several excellent ideas to keep accountable:

1) a wall chart or calendar where you mark off each day you sit down and write. ("Don't break the chain" from Jerry Seinfeld's memoir, SeinLanguage was the source of this idea.)

2) entering contests with hard deadlines

3) programming to-do lists using various apps; in no particular order TickTick, Things, Google Tasks, Any.do, Todoist.

4) doing writing prompts like NaNoWriMo (look it up, it's a November writing frenzy that you do with an online group of 5000 of your writer-peers)

5) make yourself accountable to someone: a spouse, your own kid, your writing group, a friend. Announce your goal and then follow up to let them know if you made it. Some people use social media contacts for this. Or they just post to their followers, announcing their goals and when they are met.

At Pen Parentis, we started writer-parent Meetups. Once per week, on a drop-in basis, a small group would gather and see if they achieved their goals and set new goals for the following week. If there was any time left over, we would all discuss any blocks or difficulties that anyone had faced that week and try to brainstorm collective solutions. All the above-referenced solutions to keeping yourself accountable without an agent or editor waiting for your manuscript were brainstormed in various Pen Parentis Meetups.

Need help moving on? One of our Meetup regulars who is a full-time lawyer found that he spent too much time editing and poring over his first chapters. He brilliantly enlisted a close friend to serve as a "savings bank" for his first drafts. He would send one over at the end of a week. The friend was to keep it safe. The friend was allowed to read it, but the draft was sent with the sole function that putting it "in the bank" meant our writer had to move on to the next part of the book. What a terrific idea!

There are many ways to get yourself moving forward—the most important thing is to give yourself permission to devote yourself to completing the work in progress. However, much you can achieve while still fulfilling your obligations to your family, that's how much you should try to do! Some weeks will be better, some worse, but as long as you are moving forward, you'll see that even writing just a few new sentences will allow your project to progress.

THE WRITER'S SNACK JAR

A Word About Getting an Agent

Okay people. Let's get down to basics. Do you need an agent? Their job is to sell your book for the highest amount possible to a traditional publisher, in exchange you will pay them 15% of whatever you earn. Is that what you need/want? Look back at the previous paragraph. Does your book sell itself? If so, you don't need an agent. (Though you still might want one). Shall we start at the very beginning? A very good place to start (okay, sorry for the ear worm). Let's tackle the publishing options available to you.

TRADITIONAL PUBLISHING

Positives:

- *outside validation*
- *prestige*
- *professional editors*
- *high quality production*
- *no upfront costs*
- *bookstore distribution is easier*
- *access to a marketing team*
- *possibility of advance ($$ Yay!)*
- *team to support you*
- *experts to help you understand*

Negatives:

- *low royalty rates (usually 7%-25%)*
- *must pay back advance if book doesn't sell*
- *little creative control*
- *very slow process to get to market*
- *limited marketing assistance*
- *don't always get along with team*
- *book, intellectual property rights are owned by publisher*
- *sales reporting released bi-annually (so are your royalties)*
- *high pressure deadlines for editing drafts and next title*
- *can only sell books through approved distribution channels and never direct*

SELF PUBLISHING

Positives:

- *total creative control*
- *autonomy = empowerment*
- *retain intellectual property rights*
- *high royalties (up to 70%)*
- *easier to find audience via searchable genres/topics*
- *no downside to having no readership, well except for, no readership*
- *fast turnaround and release to market*
- *real-time sales reporting is easily accessible*
- *a lot to learn but all aspects of the book are yours to manage*

Negatives:

- *figuring things out on your own or trial and error with hiring a team*
- *little validation, most prizes won't consider self-published books*
- *upfront costs required especially if you want it to look professional*
- *not easy to get bookstore distribution*
- *not easy to get reviews or blurbs*
- *literary snobs won't give self-published books a chance*
- *you have to build your own list of industry contacts*
- *burnout is common because you're handling it all on your own*

HYBRID PUBLISHING

A third option is hybrid publishing, where you receive production assistance, keep your intellectual property rights and still earn high royalties, but you have to shop around to make sure you're dealing with a reputable publisher. If you decide to work with a hybrid publisher, a good place to start is by reviewing the IBPA Hybrid Publishing Standards. LINK: **https://www.ibpa-online.org/page/hybridpublisher**

GETTING AN AGENT

Now that everything is on the table, here's how you get an agent (if you go the traditional publishing route).

Note: only some of these are tongue in cheek

1) get an MFA and go to all the classes on finding an agent or make a best friend who is a phenomenal writer and wants you to get ahead so they connect you to their agent without you asking them to do it (if you ask, you're impinging on a friendship/mentor/teacher, so don't ask—but people sometimes offer)

2) read all the blogs on the internet about finding an agent, then do the work

3) look up the people who went to college or high school with you who are now agents and take them out for drinks or bother them on Facebook Messenger or Twitter. Don't do this publicly. DM them. It's only polite. (PS: drinks/coffee/lunch are all better options than messaging. DO NOT ask them to represent you. Instead, ask for their advice and maybe they will offer to read your manuscript—I repeat it isn't polite to ask them to read your manuscript. DO have a great "elevator pitch" summarizing your novel in an exciting way that makes them want to read it. DON'T talk about the plot for more than a minute at most. Make them ask you questions.)

4) come up with a great idea for a book that sells itself and send a great query letter to a list of 30 agents—see the internet for copious examples of how to write a query letter.

5) figure out the books that are like yours, read their acknowledgement section and track down the email for the literary agent thanked in that book. Then see note 4 above. Only tell these agents how your book is different/better than the one that they already represent (and you better be right and it better be different/better). For example: you wrote a cookbook with recipes and anecdotes about growing a garden in Brooklyn and how hilarious of a disaster it was initially. Look up the editors of 1) Brooklyn cookbooks 2) humor essays about NYC 3) gardening essays 4) NYC living and 5) all editors and agents that you know in person from meeting them at various literary events like readings in the local bookstore and "how to publish" seminars. Email them explaining that your cookbook is unique because besides the successful recipes, you also have photographs of the fails—and they are hilarious. You also have a blog in which you have 4000 followers, all of whom love posting photos of their own food-fails. In fact, you developed the hashtag food-fail and Good Morning Ohio did a little segment on it last week...

It's not a science. It is throwing spaghetti at the wall until one-piece sticks perfectly. If you're going to publish traditionally, you will need to interest an editor if you are writing nonfiction, an agent if you are writing fiction (who will then get you an editor), and if you are a poet, you go directly to a publisher. Winning prizes is one way to get these people interested. Winning prizes that get you a book contract is an even easier way.

Think of an agent as a realtor. If you have a house that is in an up-and-coming neighborhood that is better than all the other homes available on the block, or a unique home that everyone wants, or even a cheap flat in a location that is in high demand, it will be easy for a realtor to sell it at a high price.

The best way to get an agent is just to write a brilliant book that says something in a way that millions of people are eager to read.

Go, write a great book!

No joke. If your book is a knockout, people will want to be in charge of selling it.

THE WRITER'S SNACK JAR

A Word About Book Tours

First of all, if you're reading about book tours, I hope this means you already have a soon-to-be-published manuscript, in which case, congratulations! You have really succeeded.

Book tours are an infinitely changing landscape. Gone are the days where the publicist takes the most minor book, lands the author an interview on a national talk show, and catapults that book to the top of the bestseller list. Nowadays, it is generally entirely the opposite: the book lands on the bestseller list, and then the publicist is able to land the author a choice interview!

That said, there is still the self-made book tour, and many authors choose to go this route.

To arrange your own book tour with a print book, call bookstores that are within easy reach of your home. Say you are a local author and offer to do a reading. Inform them on the ways they may order the book, send them a press kit (look this up on the internet so you are prepared—it is basically the resume of an author). It will be your own job to tell the local media, but newspapers, bloggers, and even TV stations are usually pretty desperate for local content that is positive, so you might get a great article written—which you will add to your press kit for farther-away bookstores and locations.

Do you write for kids? Bonus! English teachers and school librarians are always eager to present authors to their kids. Offer to talk about your writing process and about how your book got published. If you are targeting an older audience, you can do the same for public libraries, coffee shops, and local universities and colleges.

Don't forget that writing a book makes you an expert in the topic. You can offer to sit on panels or to speak at any institution that is connected with your book's topic. Did you set a romance novel at a particular restaurant? Ask to do a reading there on a slow night or host a book launch there. Is your book set on a particular college campus? Offer to read there. Fundraisers are always looking for "stars" to feature—if you live in a smaller city and especially if you live in a small town, a reading from your whale-watching fantasy book might be the perfect keynote for the huge save-the-whales campaign the local girl scout troop is hosting. Book tours are intended to grow your audience and to give you photographs and stories to spread using social media. Everyone who knows and loves you should buy your book—get out there and make new friends!

During my time at Pen Parentis, I have heard so many stories about how parents managed book tours, from moms bringing their nursing infants along on a national tour, to dads who couldn't stand being away from their infants for even a day and who therefore did zero readings while their baby was under a year old. You get to choose how much time you wish to spend away from your child. The resources that will affect this are support and money.

SUPPORT

Do you have family, is your spouse reliable, are you even a Co-parent? If you have someone you can trust with the child, then it is a question of your own level of comfort with being away from your child for however long the book tour takes. If you have far-flung friends and family, you can set up bookstore readings only in towns/cities near those homes, impose upon those friends and family to watch your child for the duration of the reading or event. Sometimes this works brilliantly, sometimes there is a lot of guilt involved—again, this depends on you and your own personality.

MONEY

Can you afford childcare? Some writers have opted to bring the child(ren) along and have someone in the hotel watch them during the reading and/ or meeting with book clubs. There are bonded sitting services that can be called upon to do this, but they are expensive. Perhaps you have a trusted partner who can be invited along for the ride to back you up on childcare. Before you bring a child to an event where you are performing ("I'm sure they won't be any problem, they'll just sit in the back and color") be sure to ask the venue if it is child appropriate. In some cases, that will be fine— sometimes they even will be delighted to have your kids along. They can be so cute in photos! But other times, the venue is not at all child appropriate—too hot, too crowded, too boring, too bright. All of these can affect any age of the child in a negative way, and you want your book tour to be about your book, not your child!

Before you bring your child, also consider what questions you are likely to be asked by the person introducing you. If this is a reading, with your six-year-old in the room, are you going to censor your comments about the book? Is it appropriate for your child? Neurosurgeons don't bring their kids to surgery, though they might bring them to the big conference in Hawaii. Also, when you are considering the cost of childcare, think in many layers— not only in terms of books sold but also new readers, fans, social media followers. Balance the cost of that sexy trip to the largest indie bookstore in Chicago where you know no one, and your friend said only two people showed up to her reading against a reading in your tiny local bookstore in your hometown in Nebraska where your mom can watch the kids and all your middle school friends still live.... Which is a more valuable use of that $350 plane fare?

Also think outside the box for childcare. If you are considering a 6-8 pm reading in Wisconsin, try to schedule it in the summer where your hired babysitter can pick up your kid at 6:00 from the venue, walk them to the playground across the street, and bring them back at 7:30 during the signing session. The same sitter in the winter will have to meet you at the hotel at 5:30 and wait until 8:30 in the same hotel. Summer would be far more fun for your kid and less money for you!

Of course, many people can't afford any childcare, much less pay for plane fare for the whole family to several locations. Not to worry! The internet is your friend. Many groups now schedule online Meetups with their favorite authors, you can do online interviews, podcasts, you can chat on Twitter or Facebook live—there are many venues for conversations with your fans, where they can even pay you, and all you have to do is spend some time in front of your computer's camera. See you at the next Zoom meeting with your book club drinking chardonnay and talking about your wonderful words!

Just don't try to fool yourself that you can do this easily from home if your kid is also home and awake. Remember that viral video of the guy whose toddler interrupted his nationally televised interview; and try to find a playdate or support sitter for the hour that you'll be busy. The iPad is good at occupying kids for a short while but expect to be called away at some point if there's not another person around to run some interference.

Don't worry. Everyone is used to this by now. Just be gracious and as brief as possible and don't forget to mute while you duck out of frame.

THE WRITER'S SNACK JAR

A Word About the Corpse in The Sink

When we were first considering a Pen Parentis book, a Denver-based poet with two kids, Mary Harpin, spent two years interviewing dozens of parent writers for Pen Parentis to discover how they managed their resources and what their specific struggles had been. She is a published poet, an intuitive development instructor, and a content writer for Fortune 500 medical device companies. (Shadowrise, her debut collection of poetry, was released by Dos Madres Press in November of 2019, and you can read more about her excellent work at maryharpin.com)

Although we were unable to collect enough responses to allow for scientific statistical significance, we decided that having more than a hundred survey responses could still give some insight into the private struggles and triumphs of people who write with kids living at home. The data offers some surprises, some help, and some confirmation of conflicts we suspected were common but were never quite sure. I asked her to write up our results for this book and she sent this fantastic essay, leading with the quote from Anne Lamott from Bird by Bird:

"I used to not be able to work if there were dishes in the sink.
Then I had a child and now I can work if there is a corpse in the sink."

Mary Harpin's Writer-Parent Survey Findings

"Several years ago, I was working a part-time consulting gig and trying to write a poetry book while mothering a one and 4-year-old. The writing project was stalled. Actually, it was worse than stalling, it was regressing. I would force domestic duties aside only to feel too scattered and guilty to make real progress on my poetry.

In the few hours I'd manage to remove myself from interruptions, I would stare bleary-eyed at the screen and begin editing, only to return later, disappointed with my changes, and reverse it all. Having lived in Denver for just a few years, my community was small. The gulf between my two selves — the pre-kid creative-me and the post-kid-creative-me — grew broader and more profound.

Parents who could write and publish productively, especially with small children, baffled me. Tired and disconnected from my fellow writers and parents, I wanted advice, but advice felt cliché and disconnected. "Write poems on the back of a receipt while you're waiting in the carpool line!" or "Wake up 2 hours earlier and don't let anyone interrupt you!"

If what worked for other people wasn't quite right for me, what was right for me? Was I a stay-up-later writer? Was I a write-while-they-nap person? Did I need to join a group? Hire a coach? I didn't know where to start.

I connected with Pen Parentis to simply ask writer-parents what works for them and what doesn't, and to find out how they feel and how their productivity changes as their children grow. Together, we conducted in-depth interviews with dozens of writers who have kids and then ran a qualitative and quantitative survey of 132 others who volunteered to fill out our lengthy questionnaire.

I didn't know it then, but the bleariness I felt—that lack of "brain space"—was a significant hurdle for most of the writers we interviewed and surveyed for this project. My assumption was that writers would report a lack of time as their greatest obstacle, and it made the short list. But it's more complex than that.

Writers (creatives I suspect) work well when they're in the flow, the state where we're so absorbed in the act of creation that we lose a sense of time and surroundings. When I'm in the flow-state, there's a perceivable shift in consciousness. I am ultra-present, focused and clear, and that contributes to the quality of my work, the pleasure I take in it, and the relief and satisfaction I feel having created.

That ability to find a flow is what felt so distant and inaccessible to me when I became a parent, both due to constant interruption, lack of time, but largely the lack of mental clarity that happens when you're overwhelmed and tired.

The work-around, it appears, is not to create the perfect circumstances to reach a flow state, it's to figure out how to have children and the resulting mental fatigue and get there anyway. Then, when your kids' needs change in what feels like two seconds later, recalibrate to find flow again.

The intention behind our survey was to find out how that is done. I found answers to some of those big questions, as well as the comfort of knowing that very few parents (only 19%) feel like they have all the resources they need to support their creative writing life. Yet they make progress anyway. There are also clear benefits that only becoming a parent can offer.

Sixty-five percent of the people we surveyed feel strongly that becoming a parent has enriched their writing and creative lives. Most feel proud to show their children how satisfying and essential a creative life is. Many feel they've become even more productive, focused, and efficient as writers. One parent wrote:

> **"I love that my kids know that writing and creating books is important to me. I love that my eldest daughter now says that when she grows up, she wants to be "A [mom] and a comic book creator," and that she does not see the conflict between the two... Engaging in and doing the creative work is both revitalizing and enriching, and I believe it gives me energy for parenting."**

There is a myriad of life situations reflected in the data we collected, from parents with or without partner support, from those with trust funds to those with revolving debt, from those with supportive communities to those who feel isolated. In my situation, I have a supportive spouse and earn a living as a contract content writer for businesses part time. I've arranged and re-arranged my paid work with an amount of childcare to figure out how to find writing time. To finish my book, I put things on hold... reluctantly, including my work for Pen Parentis. It's no coincidence that my book was accepted for publication the same year my youngest daughter went to kindergarten.

Our respondents shared frustrations, successes, and a list of the things they sacrificed. They also shared hope, personal satisfaction, and commitment to what they see not as a job not as a hobby, but as a vocation."

Below, I summarize what our 132 respondents said, and I hope that whether you're in the place Mary was several years ago (bleary and baffled and feeling like somehow everyone was figuring it out except for her), you'll be able to take something away from the data that Mary has analyzed below and we both hope this will inspire you or help you or at the very least, make you feel less alone.

Some Notes and Disclaimers

Mary Harpin worked very hard on this study, consulting two professional academic researchers to help craft questions and crunch numbers, but be aware that this study doesn't follow all the strict protocols of a rigorous, official, blessed by-peer-review academic study. It's designed to show trends and tell stories, to round up feelings, thoughts, and answers that writers may not always readily share in everyday interactions. Percentages below are rounded to the nearest whole number.

Who took the survey?

- Of the 132 respondents, nearly 80% identify as female; we had 1 non-binary participant and the rest identify as male.
- About 70% had a book or more forthcoming or published. (All were published professionally somewhere.)
- About 80% of these with books lived with a spouse or partner, and all had at least one child living at home.
- 36% live in a large urban area. 11% live in a rural area. The rest live in suburbs, small cities or towns.

How Did Things Change in Writers' Lives After Kids?

Parent writers felt that creative idea generation and pleasure in writing stayed the same after having children. While they reported less time to write, the time they had was more efficient, and the quality of their work had improved. Most respondents wrote about 5-10 hours per week, more often several hours at a time rather than inter-spaced throughout the day or week. The number one challenge wasn't time or money; it was emotional brain space. Feeling too mentally fried keeps parents from writing as much as they'd like.

Since having kids:

38% said they feel their submitting and publishing efforts improved

37% feel their productivity has improved or stayed the same

39% feel like their ability to advance professionally as a writer has improved or stayed the same

50% feel that they are more efficient with their writing time

51% feel that their drive to continue writing has increased

58% feel that the quality of their work has improved

YET:

- 76% say they struggle to find the emotional brain-space to write

What gives?

Parents suggest that they felt more at peace when they accepted that writing time would usually cost something, whether that's sleep or quality time or something else. One wrote, "Be intensely conscious of the opportunity cost of whatever you're not doing, and make sure what you're doing is worth that cost."

Parents report giving up these things "sometimes" or "often" to write:

- Kid time: 79%
- Sleep: 82%
- Partner time: 86%
- Domestic maintenance: 93%
- Leisure time: 97%

Finances & Income

Most respondents work outside the home in some capacity, and about half use their writing skills in their day job to some extent.

- 46% work
- 37% work full-time outside the home
- 32% report that writing expenses cost more than they earn from writing (23% break-even)
- 32% earn up to a quarter of their income from writing
- 12% earn half-to-all of their income from writing
- 47% always or sometimes carry revolving debt to cover writing-related expenses
- 60% say they are not bringing in the income they'd like to earn from writing

Limitations & Support

The primary reason writers feel limited in their work is lack of time, and usually they let the housework, sleep, or time with their partner slide. Lack of time and lack of rest lead to the feeling of being fried. They frequently feel limited by a day-job schedule (56%), need for money (55%), and lack of childcare (43%). About 24% feel that outdated gender roles limit their writing.

What helps?

The most helpful external resources that support their writing life were:

- 73%: A supportive partner
- 59%: Income from a spouse or partner
- 33%: A good day job
- 28%: Helpful extended family
- 13%: Free or low-cost childcare
- 20%: Helpful friends/neighbors
- 11%: Passive Income

Tips from Respondents

(Grammar has been corrected in these anonymously submitted quotes.)

- *Stop thinking about it and let it all flow together. Do not pick up work that other family members ignore. Hold them accountable and accept the consequences of disorder.*

- *In my experience, partners are often more difficult to balance than parenting because most adults find creative work that does not make money hard to understand as essential. Staying single as a parent has given me more control over both my work time and my child intensive time, as well as allowed me to maintain faith in the value of poetic work, but it's lonely. Good friends who are also single parenting creatives have been my rock!*

- *Keep breathing; children are a creative act, important in making me who I am and therefore making me the artist I am.*

- *It's okay to have an untidy house. It's okay to leave dishes in the sink. It's okay to force your hubby and kids to get their own laundry out of the dryer. Domestic shit can eat into writing time more than almost anything else save childcare. Once kids are in the school system, it gets easier. I had to stay up until 3 am to write when my kids were infants and toddlers. Once they got into elementary, everything changed.*

- *It's never going to feel like you're doing everything right. Never. But that's okay, it's just what it feels like and not what's actually happening. Try not to compare what's going on in your writing life with what appears to be happening in the lives of non-parent writers. As long as you're moving forward, you're still getting somewhere.*

- Be willing to let certain things go where children are concerned.

- Learn how to set reasonable goals so that you don't punish yourself for failing to meet unreasonable ones. Expect and embrace interruptions.

- If you want to make the creative writing life work, you absolutely have to carve out the time and stick to it, no matter what. Of course, some things will crop up (a hospitalized family member, weddings/funerals, pre-planned family vacations). But whenever possible, keep that writing time sacred.

- The only way to balance the unbalanced is to accept that something will get set aside. My family comes first, and even if I don't love that, I have to accept it.

- You have to bring your child into the process: your child needs to understand that your writing is part of what makes mommy or daddy who and what they are, and that leading a purpose-driven life is important. If the child understands that, the time you need away from them to write doesn't seem punitive. Also, remember the post-it note Philip Roth taped to his computer: "Stay Put."

- Don't be afraid to ask for help. Don't be scared to say no to other people.

- Finding some sort of accountability to a group or a coach helps significantly. Keeping my eye on deadlines for submitting to workshops where I meet and work with other writers is also crucial for helping me keep my focus during the rest of the year.

- Creating a supportive community of writers and friends and stick with it. Balance writing time and be flexible, but also committed. Look to your children for inspiration and be a role model for them by achieving your dreams. Obstacles and challenges will happen. Remember to find a comfortable pace and stick with it. Find your regular time to write (however long) and stick with it; be flexible but committed, at whatever pace you can manage.

- I think it's important to set goals but remain flexible in how you'll achieve them. It's also crucial not to fall into despair when you feel like you haven't produced as much as you'd like.

Inspiration from Respondents

"On one hand, having kids has definitely enriched my creative life in that it's taken me into projects and to places I never would have thought to go otherwise. On the other hand, it's a lot, it's always a lot, and there's less time to actually do the work, which means everything slows down."

"The struggles and challenges that have happened in the past 7 years have refueled my passion and strengthened my writing voice. I also feel like being away from it has made me desperate to write anything, whatever comes to mind. And that has returned me to writing for the love of it."

"Becoming a parent refined me as a writer. Sure, it took away my time to create, but now I create with verve and purpose."

"It's not easy but I like to share what I do with my kids now and they are starting to appreciate that I am a writer, not just a mom. They are also making up their own stories, which is great."

"Being a parent lends itself to a much deeper understanding of thoughts and feelings I only partially knew before. It makes writing a much more special thing to me."

"Becoming a mother makes you more attuned to the development of a person. You can use that to develop your characters or imagine where they come from. Children teach you a lot, every day, at every stage of their growth. Listen and use that information in your writing."

"My kids give me my best material."

"There is always a way to make a writing career happen. Send what you want out to the world. You'll find grants, opportunities, help with submissions and rejections, with revisions."

"Put aside money, whatever you can, to invest in yourself going to conferences and hiring a coach or an editor if you need one."

"Just don't quit. Even when it seems like you really should smash your computer, burn your journals, break your fingers, don't. Your creative voice is yours and yours alone, meant to be shared and honored. Do that for yourself and as an example for your children."

"It's hard, but I'm glad I keep trying."

"I'm a better writer because of my children."

THE WRITER'S SNACK JAR

An Unexpected Word About Coronavirus

So, I wrote this whole book in 2019 and then in 2020 the freaking world blew up with fire tornadoes, murderous hornets, hellish hurricanes, infernal fires, attack hippos, possible aliens, impossible heat waves, and of course, Covid-19.

I don't know what to tell you. Unanticipated, to say the least. A lot of the advice I give and relate in this book is from an earlier, easier time when parents could eventually rely on six hours of school to watch their kids and could go to a coffee shop in a thunderstorm and work there for an hour or two as long as their laptop battery held out.

Now? These solutions are entirely up in the air.

I will tell you that at Pen Parentis, the weekly online accountability Meetups on zoom are the only thing keeping some of our members on creative track. The frequency with which our members say "I would never have written this chapter, but I told the group I would do it so last night I was up until 1am writing"... it is astonishing how many pages have been written just so that these parents could proudly say they achieved their self-appointed goals.

So, while I can't make sweeping proclamations anymore, I can tell you that as a Pen Parentis member, the things that can get you through being quarantined with your kids are:

1) **Join an accountability group.** If you can't afford it, we will find a way to make it affordable to you. If you really can't afford even $10/month, we have a weekly check-in on Facebook that we welcome you to use like our in-person zooms. Set a goal, announce it to the group and then the next week let us know if you achieved it. Hopefully, the libraries will have reopened and everyone is able to access a computer once per week.

2) **Watch the archived videos of Dr. Michelle Tichy.** There have been two talkbacks as of this writing, and both are available online on our Pen Parentis YouTube channel. She is an expert on holistic family happiness when children are homeschooled with working-from-home parents and both of the talkbacks center solidly on issues faced by writer-parents quarantined with their kids.

3) **Take good care of yourself, mentally and physically.** If you are happy, your children will be happier. If writing makes you happy, find a way to work it into your life. If writing stresses you out, maybe stop being so hard on yourself.

In general, be a little less demanding of yourself.
Your kids need love.
You also need love. Your writing will flow
when you can get some mental space.
Keep your skills primed.

As I said recently on Twitter to a wonderful writer with kids who complained she had hit a wall, "Hang in there and gather your strength. When that wall crumbles—as all walls do—be ready to use the momentum to fly."

THE WRITER'S SNACK JAR

Community, The Most Valuable Resource
(A long and worthwhile read)

You need this.

You'll probably be surprised to learn that when I started a graduate school for writing I was a loner. I had a do-it-yourself mentality that some people might call stubborn insistence and others might call a chip on my shoulder. In my extreme naivete, I kept turning down opportunities, insisting that I did not want a career boost from my peers—I believed I was in graduate school to be taught, not to learn. I was eager to be edited, but reluctant to be published. The idea of a friend who worked on a literary journal telling me to submit there made me cringe! Now I know that they weren't suggesting they could make it easier for me to get in, they just wanted to let me know that submissions were open. But I had weird ideas and wanted to do everything on my own, without relying on the kindness of others. Even now my writing group teases me because I don't want to hear their praise, I want to jump right into where the writing can be improved! But in looking so narrowly at what it means to be helped, I was missing a very important part of what it means to be a writer.

Writers are part of a vast interconnected system. Writers function as editors, teachers, researchers, developers, content creators, sensitivity readers, scriptwriters, publishers, agents, and a score of other careers. It is just as easy to become a bestselling writer if you are first an agent as it is to become a high-powered agent after being a bestselling writer! (Do take note that neither is actually easy.) My point is that traditional publishing is about creating a product that people want to read. So, you could become a celebrity and then publishers will clamor for you to publish a story. Or you could be a ghostwriter hired to write that celebrity's story. There are infinite paths to publication - but all of them require connection to other people. Even if you self-publish, you'll need to know how to do it, where to do it, how to make sure you're not being scammed, you'll need to know about distribution, and then you'll want to know people who can write reviews for you. You are not an island. No one is.

On my first day in Helen Schulman's writing workshop at Columbia, she leaned back in her chair and said, "look to your left and your right. That, my friends, is what your MFA program can give you. This is the value of your education. These people. All the people in this room are writers. All of them will be your forever-editors, your friends, your support system. When you are looking for blurbs, these are the people who will write them for you. When you are looking for work, these are the people who will be agents, editors, and small publishers. You don't have to write a single great word while you are at Columbia, so long as you make great friends."

I didn't listen to her at the time, but despite my reluctance to heed good advice, I did make long-lasting friendships in my MFA program. And Helen was right. Many of the people in that classroom have become striking literary figures. Impressively so.

A decade after the first Pen Parentis After Work Reading, I was invited to a writers' forum in Lithuania. It was the inaugural Lithuanian Writers of the Diaspora Forum and marked the first time I had ever been invited as a writing professional to appear in public, even though I had been Co-hosting salons every month for ten years!

I wrote about this life-altering experience soon after my return:

Six of us, all Lithuanian-heritage writers from different lands, were invited by the Lithuanian Ministry of Education and Science to make a special, extra trip to visit some local high schools and meet with their writing classes. I jumped at the chance as I had a teenager of my own and wanted to do some covert comparative sociological research on global teen cellphone use and attitudes towards authority. I found myself assigned to Vytauto Didžiojo High School, one of the top-ranked public schools in the capital city. A driver would pick us up at 8:45am. Sharp.

A ratty 1980s-style school bus pulled up promptly at 8:44am. Many of us were leaving directly from these visits to airports for overseas flights home, but the driver refused to touch our oversized bags. He stood by, arms crossed, not even twitching to help, as six well-heeled women hefted monstrous luggage into the back of the bus.

Clearly, his job was driver, not valet.

He jerked the yellow bus into gear, and we were off on our adventure. The representative from the government would be meeting us at the various schools. We chattered animatedly about what we could expect and what we hoped to learn and teach. Some of us had made lesson plans, others, like me, were expecting to simply answer questions from the high school kids. My class, I had been informed, would want to speak in English.

The bus inched down a cobblestone alley barely as wide as the vehicle.

"Okay," said the driver in Lithuanian with a strong Russian accent, rubbing his military haircut, "I see the school from here. You'll have to walk. I don't know how to get there."

I pulled out my phone to do a map search–in fact we were a whole winding route away from where we needed to be, though the rooftop of the school was indeed visible–across a locked courtyard. A gentle woman from Spain started to pack up her luggage to walk by and I stopped her.

"We can't get there from here," I told the driver, pointing out the locked gate between us and the back of the school. "You have to drive us closer."

"I don't know where to go," said the driver.

I was sorely tempted to let him know that my job was to be a featured presenter, not a driver—but I am not that sort. I showed the map to my new friends, one of them got out and we flagged down a mom behind us who wanted to turn into a different locked courtyard. She and the driver had a short conversation (I overheard, "I don't know where to drive" and "I'm telling you where to drive") and at last we drove around a corner to the front of the school, where there were two young students eagerly waiting for us at the front door. They grabbed our bags and guided us to the principal's office where more students had been drafted into being our guides for the day (mine was a soft-spoken redheaded junior who spoke three languages fluently and secretly confided to me that she, too, had once believed that all kids spoke a different language at home than in public—she incidentally had to take a math exam during her day, which she did in the back of one of the English classrooms where I was presenting, without complaint.)

I met a wonderful English teacher, Goda, who spoke with a British accent and explained to me she was still teaching her kids conditional clauses, but that she thought they would be perfectly capable of communicating with me in English. What she wanted was for the kids to have the freedom to ask me anything. I was all in and descended upon the classroom happy to strike up any conversation.

The kids were sleepy-eyed, muted—as kids in schools always seem to be. They moved indifferently, with only the tiniest spark of interest when they saw a new person in the room. I was myself: chatty, probably too loud, animated. Soon three or four of the ten kids perked up. I was clearly unusual. I saw disbelieving glances smiles of "what the hell is this?" And before the class had fully started, all of them had put their cellphones away and were paying attention, either eagerly with great openness or cagily as if worried that I might bite.

The questions began: "What is it like in NYC?" "How are American teenagers different from us?" "What is the difference between Target and Walmart?" Wonderful questions that they really wanted to know the answers to.

And then came a question that showed me how differently writers and artists were considered in this country: "What are your hobbies?"

I have never been at any writing event where the author was asked about her hobbies. In fact, most of the United States thinks of writing itself as a hobby. These kids wanted to know if I did crossword puzzles or jigsaw puzzles (I do) or fished or gardened (I don't.) They wanted to see me as a whole person. They wanted to know about my children, my personal life, the foods I liked to eat, and the season I preferred. For them, writing was a career that passionate and talented people chose. It was not an outsider choice that bore any scrutiny. It was a calling.

"Do you write from pain or from love?"

"What is the theme that you most often write about?"

"What is the piece of your own writing that you love the most, and why?"

These were deep and intense questions, questions I wanted to answer over cocktails with hours to discuss. I had an hour and had to move on to the next classroom. It was, to be honest, magical.

But the most life-affirming moment of the school visit happened two days after I returned to the States. I was prepping for the Grand Finale of the 10th Anniversary season of Pen Parentis Literary Salons. I had happened to mention the organization in my bio, and Goda the English teacher had in the meantime looked it up on the internet.

"Hey hey, hallo Milda," she wrote in an email. She thanked me for coming and for my openness and energy— "the students loved you because you were so emotional and free! They did not notice how tight and reserved they had become..." Goda went on to detail a few moments that had stood out for her and her students and then she wrote about how sorry she felt to not have the support that Pen Parentis members get... She said that it might be a post-Soviet legacy, but every writer and artist is on their own in her country, figuring everything out their own way. They enjoy all the possible rights one can get, lots of freedom for expression and creativity, but there in their creative lives, they are most alone.

And that was when it hit me, what we have here. We have community. We have support. Pen Parentis created a new way for creative people to come together–if you are a writer and a parent, you are included. We look only at our commonalities, expecting that to bind us together—we know we all have differences, and that we are all individuals. We respect and admire our differences, but what makes us strong is that we all have similarities as well.

It changed my life to recognize this openly. Inclusivity is one of our core values (the four are: inclusivity, community, balance and professionalism)– it is a rare gift and one that we could do well to celebrate more often.

I started Pen Parentis with the idea that there had to be others like me out there, and that I could learn by example. In the beginning, there were no plans to make our little reading series into a collective or start up a business or organization. We just wanted to hear how other writers had managed to write a book, despite having kids. We started The Pen Parentis After Work Reading Series (our first name was Pens and Pacifiers, but we were afraid to limit ourselves to just babies for fear of running out of writers to present!) with joy and hope that we would meet people who could talk about the experience of being a writer parent and let us know a little of how they overcame the difficulties in their own lives. It was meant to build community, to share experience. It wasn't formed to last, just to help anyone who needed help at the time.

From the beginning, the reading series was about acceptance. My Co-hosts and I don't judge — we learn. Sometimes we commiserate. Sometimes sympathize. The readings are top-quality, have been since the beginning, and the Q&A that follows is sometimes so raw or so funny or so unexpected, that truly magical things happen.

What I have learned in ten years of hosting salons, bringing writer-parents together in Meetups and special events, and watching writers win Fellowships, is that everyone has a story and the only through-line is that these writers kept going. Some of them had writer's block for months or even years. Some had children with medical issues that outweighed the parenting dilemmas. Some had horrible things occur: the death of children, the death of spouses, financial ruin, fires, and many unexpected divorces. But these writers eventually got back to writing. They wrote. They sent out. They published. They started the entire process all over again.

And it was never easy.

After each of our initial events, we were overwhelmed by a tidal wave of positive feedback. The writers were amazed at the notion that anyone would publicly value the sacrifices they had made to maintain their writing careers. The audiences could not get enough of the stories that the writers told once they were featured as human beings and not just marketing tools for their books. We knew we had a terrific reading series on our hands, but the leap to turning that into an official organization took the vision of an up-and-coming corporate lawyer named Laura Rose Bloxham.

I had made the decision to turn the reading series into a company and to my dismay, the curator and Co-host who had helped start the reading series turned down my offer of signing on as a limited partnership. She was actively house hunting while parenting two very young boys and writing a book—she wanted to step away from curating and didn't have space for a new business in her life. She wished me well but respectfully declined any involvement in a business, so I took a few online classes and went out and got a DBA as a sole proprietor. I opened a bank account for the new company, and then found a fiscal sponsor, Fractured Atlas, so I could take tax-deductible donations on behalf of Pen Parentis.

Enter Laura. She approached me after a salon and suggested that her highly esteemed law firm (Milbank Tweed Hadley and McCloy) help me get a 501c3 and turn Pen Parentis into an actual nonprofit company. This was pro-bono help of the highest caliber, and I was delighted to accept the help.

Thus, (insert drumroll and cymbal crash here, and fireworks and a round of applause) with the aid of my colleagues Emily Speer Ryan (who had all the business acumen I lacked and agreed to serve as the first Board Treasurer) and Michael Del Castillo (who had the experience of running a nonprofit I lacked, and was the Secretary to my Presidency on the first-ever Executive Board), in December 2014, Pen Parentis, Ltd, was born.

Now it's 2019 and our Executive Board is the largest it has ever been:

Our long-terms members
Jamie Baletti Clarke (one of our very first salon attendees, and one of my oldest friends.)
Laura Rose Bloxham (remember the lawyer who was our fairy godmother?)
Arlaina Tibensky (our first curator)
Christina Chiu (our current curator as of 2019)
Renee Simms (who read at a Salon and is an educator and a writer)
Emily Speer Ryan has been a long-time member of the Board

Our new-comers
Julie Paddleford
Helen Wan
Helene Epstein

And me. I passed the hat of President to Marina Aris who wears it with great panache. It is an exciting time for Pen Parentis—forward facing with great strides to make. We are eager to see what the future brings to this little literary nonprofit.

The Grand Finale of our tenth anniversary season was held in the Oculus at Westfield World Trade Center. You have to understand, part of the reason the reading series is in Downtown Manhattan is that I live down here. My husband and I bought our first home just after I graduated from Columbia in May 2001—and the apartment was just a block away from the World Trade Center with its wonderful Twin Towers.

Did a little shudder run up your spine? Yes. We bought our first place and spent the whole summer enthralled by the River-to-River Festival, and the various international dance festivals were always in play in and around the World Trade Center plaza. I spent the entire summer learning the neighborhood, memorizing the mall, and walking the riverfront. In September of that same year, less than four months after we moved downtown, tragedy hit, and our lives were permanently altered. We refused to leave, instead latching on to the hopeful rebuild and renew campaigns that LMHQ was spearheading.

We welcomed our son in 2002 and our daughter in 2006. By 2008, I was beyond ready to have the arts return to our neighborhood - and I was willing to become a catalyst to make that happen. The Pen Parentis After-Work Reading Series started in 2009 and was intended to bring literature back to the community where my beloved three-story Borders Bookstore had been crushed under the weight of a building and an airplane. In fact, I forged a partnership with Borders when it reopened at 100 Broadway (ironically, their new store occupied the very lobby where I had my first job in New York City: as a receptionist in the Bank of Tokyo Trust Company) — Borders distributed books at our Salons until the corporation shut its doors permanently in 2011.

Do I regret spending ten years of my life on something that doesn't pay me, putting off my own creative writing to the wee hours of the night in favor of grant writing all day?

Can't say I regret a thing.

I never looked back. Community. I was certain that it could make a difference in people's lives. Pen Parentis proves this every day. There isn't a single day where some writer doesn't text, tweet, email, Linked In comment, Facebook Like, Instagram heart, fill out our online contact us form, or write an actual letter on cardstock praising our work. Nearly every card says the same thing either long form or in just a few words, and reading these words, I always feel that we have succeeded. What they all say is this:

Thank you for existing. Pen Parentis matters to me. Someday, I hope it matters to the whole world.

THE WRITER'S SNACK JAR

The Last Word

As a parent, you are fully connected to history. You understand a human's place in the long string of those who came before and those who will come after. You can comprehend that parenting decisions are surprisingly off-the-cuff, sometimes even the most life-altering decisions are made in the heat of a moment. This will bode you well when your character needs to leave a room and you can't figure out how to get them out that door. While you may never entirely forgive your own parents for their flaws, at least you can begin to empathize with how difficult every parent's road can be.

Guilt is your biggest enemy. Guilt can stop you from writing even when you have found a way to carve out some time, have gotten enough sleep, the kid-issues are resolved, and you have (for the moment) enough money to feel okay. Guilt can still knock you silly.

Try to remember that there are no rules about doing this. None. Each kid is an individual and each parenting situation is unique. You would scoff at a book that told you "How to Have a Perfect Marriage" (even though you might buy it) because you know in your heart that every relationship is unique and if someone gave you step-by-step instructions on how much time together is enough, and who should be doing which chores and who should be earning most of the money and how many intimate moments are enough to sustain a "good" marriage, it would be ridiculous posturing. So why do we all feel that there is some "right" way to parent?

Benevolent neglect all the way to snowplow parenting: all of it is simply what some parent thought would work best for their family at that moment in time. You will find yourself in situations where you have done just about everything on the spectrum. That's okay. We are all striving to do our best at any given moment. Kids are designed to want more (all humans are)–so remember yourself and your needs. Find a community that supports those needs and see what works for them. See if those tips will work for you.

If you want your child to remember you as a writer, you have to actually write.

USE:

- *your newfound empathy to enrich your invented characters.*
- *the miracle of birth to remind yourself to continue to create, no matter how impossible.*
- *the cognitive dissonances of the panic and joy and love and despair of new parenthood.*
- *the overwhelming delight and keen observational powers of a toddler.*
- *the impossible stubbornness and powerful self-confidence of the young child.*
- *the fierce independence, extraordinary mistakes, and daring self-reliance of the teen.*
- *the vulnerable secret terror and beautiful, well-deserved pride of the new adult.*

All of this is your material. All of this will be at your fingertips whether you write one-room cozy mysteries or flowery historical romances or Pulitzer Prize-nominated sprawling novels of ideas. Use it.

As we say here:

Parenting done, write.

OFFERINGS FOR PEN PARENTIS
TITLE MEMBERS*

Writing Fellowship for New Parents

- To encourage writers with children under 10 to create new, professional-quality fiction, entry fee waived

- $1000 prize, one year of mentorship and unlimited access to Pen Parentis programs, international publication through partnership with Dreamers Creative Writing magazine. Participation in a Pen Parentis Literary Salon alongside established authors who are also parents.

Literary Salons

- Themed and moderated roundtables of small groups of authors who are also parents

- Published or prize-winning Title Members can participate on the panels—broadcast on social media to the general public

  - Second Tuesday of each month, September through May

  - In partnership with McNally Jackson Bookstore – in-person events will resume in their downtown New York City location at the South Street Seaport as soon as the pandemic restrictions ease

  - Archives of entire salons are available on You Tube (YouTube. com/penparentis)

- Archives also available in edited 20 minute segments on IGTV (Instagram.com/penparentis)

- Unedited raw footage is available on Facebook (Facebook.com/penparentis)

- Intimate interviews with many of the authors featured at our salons are available in print on our website (penparentis.org/interviews)

- Unpublished and emerging members are encouraged to participate from the audience, ask questions, and volunteer comments.

Cycle of Support

MENTORSHIP: available free through our Facebook group, just click the mentorship tab and apply to be a mentor or mentee. Facebook.com/groups/penparentis

MEMBERSHIP: various levels, PBS-style, based on your ability to pay. You start or stop at anytime. Publicity, opportunities, discounts with high-quality partners such as One Lit Place, Paragraph Writing Space, and the new writing residency Scribente Maternum.

MEETUPS: creating small supportive groups of writers (who are parents) that meet weekly to discuss craft, pool resources, and set goals to measure progress on individual writing goals. These have resulted in Cheerleading Text Chains, Night Write "night sessions" in homes across the country, Workshops and partnerships. Title Members can volunteer to lead groups or join an existing group.

Annual AWP Meetup – in addition to providing tips on how to attend a conference if you have kids, when this conference is in person, Pen Parentis hosts a National Meetup for Writer-Parents open to any writer who has kids. Frequently, high-profile writers who have been featured at Pen Parentis Literary Salons make appearances at this event. (AWP 2021 – Pen Parentis hosts an online "bookfair space" full of activities for kids of writers, so that the writers themselves can attend panels or networking sessions)

ANNEX ACTIVITIES:

- Access to publishing opportunities

- Member-curated list of writing residencies and colonies that feature benefits exclusive to parents

- List of "side-gigs" – various writing-related services that members offer, frequently at a discount to other members.

- Pen Parentis Behind Closed Doors – Facebook group with discussions about writing, publishing, and parenthood while writing.

- Linked In Group – similar to Facebook group but with a target to sharing online resources for writers.

- @PenParentis on Twitter (#readatPenParentis, #parentingdonewrite) – promotion for writers who are also parents, opportunities, and job listings.

- @PenParentis on Instagram (#readatPenParentis) – up to the minute listings of opportunities for writers who are parents

- @PenParentis on LinkedIn – featuring larger announcements by writers who #readatPenParentis like national and international prizes

POCKET PEN – free app on both Apple and Android platforms which gathers "stolen" writing time (you can email these jotted notes to yourself or save them on the app) and tracks the amount you have written by tallying these microsessions up on your behalf

BOOK CLUB – online discussion of writing craft books

SPECIAL EVENTS: frequent one-off sessions addressing current needs of writers who are parents

PANEL DISCUSSIONS: various panels including "Turning Discouragement into Productivity" led by Christina Chiu, "Privacy Matters: Sell your Book, Not your Baby," led by M. M. De Voe, and forthcoming - "Author Mom Self-Care," led by Carla DuPree.

BOOKS AHOY! A day-long celebration of children's literature aboard an historical boat (with mermaids and pirates) for kids of all ages

HIGH NOTES: a rooftop celebration of writing and music inspired by the written word

OUT LOUD: training session by actors for writers on how to do public readings

HOUSE OF LIT PARTY: a collaboration with Mutha magazine, a whole day of events celebrating story and creativity for the whole family in an historical house on Governor's Island in NYC.

SANITY LUNCH: zoom session with educational psychologist and social justice advocate Dr. Michelle Tichy addressing the various needs of families quarantined together with kids of various ages – when everyone in the family needs to get work done and the kids have online school.

*Title Members commit to a low monthly donation and are allowed free unlimited access to all of these benefits. Basic Membership to Pen Parentis is free and many of these benefits are also included, though some come at a low per-use fee. Donations to Pen Parentis are tax deductible under federal 501c3 guidelines.

Join Pen Parentis!
https://www.penparentis.org/where-you-come-inbecome-a-member/

THE WRITER'S SNACK JAR

Pen Parentis Salon Authors
2009–2019
(Listed in alphabetical order)

A

Lauren Acampora

André Aciman

Thelma Adams

Siobhan Adcock

Rumaan Alam

Elisa Albert

Huda Al-Marashi

Will Allison

Tara Altebrando

Marika Alzadon

Sam Apple

Gint Aras

James Arthur

B

Rebecca Barry

Cathleen Bell

Jennifer Belle

Helen Benedict

Miranda Beverly-Whittemore

Randon Billings Noble

L. Annette Binder

Robin Black

Keith Blanchard

Paula Bomer

Marguerite Bouvard

Jamie Brenner

Mahogany Browne

Marina Budhos

Granville Wythe Burgess

John Burnham-Schwartz

C

Will Chancellor

Pang-Mei Natasha Chang

Tina Chang

Ava Chin

Wendy Chin-Tanner

Jennifer Cody Epstein

Myfanwy Collins

Matt Costello

Lydia Cortes

Aleksandra Crapanzano

Victor Cruz

Sonja Curry-Johnson

Kathy Curto

D

Michael Dahlie

Susan Daitch

Victoria Z Daly

Patty Dann

Marcy Dermansky

Kristen Dollard

Tim Donnelly

Aidan Donnelley Rowley

John Donohue

Larry Doyle

Amy Dryansky

Jamie Duclos-Yourdon

Patricia Dunn

Carla Du Pree

E

David Ebenbach

Amy Edwards

Janice Eidus

Jennifer Egan

Nic Esposito

F

Herta Feely

Stephanie Feldman

Sean Ferrell

Miranda Field

Julia Fierro

Tim Fitts

Jennifer Fliss

Nick Flynn

Thaisa Frank

Gabriel Fried

Tad Friend

Andrew Friedman

John Freeman Gill

G

Eleni Gage

Jonathan Galassi

Sarah Gambito

Sarah Gardner Borden

Elana Gartner

Diana Geffner-Ventura

Sarah Gerkensmeyer

David Gilbert

Shani Raine Gilchrist

Elizabeth Isadora Gold

Caroline Grant

Michael Greenburg

Karl Taro Greenfeld

Ben Greenman

Brian Gresko

Lauren Grodstein

Lewis Gross

Lev Grossman

H

Jessica Hagedorn

Ted Hamm

Jimin Han

Frank Haberle

Jennifer Michael Hecht

Jared Harél

Virginia Hartman
Eleanor Henderson
Joshua Henkin
Patricia Henley
Joanna Hershon
Jess deCourcy Hinds
Nancy Hoch
Cara Hoffman
Ann Hood
JP Howard
Marie Howe

J

Mira Jacob
Joanne Jacobson
Karl Jacoby
Lori Jakiela
Kristopher Jansma
Gish Jen
John Jodzio

K

Elizabeth Kadetsky
Amelia Kahaney
Sarah Kain Gutowski
Alice Kaltman
Jessica Kane
Roy Kersey
Julie Klam
Deborah Kogan

Anne Korkeakivi

Nicola Kraus

Kara Krauze

Heather Kristin

Keetje Kuipers

Amitava Kumar

L

Ben Lahring

John Langan

Sarah Langan

Victor LaValle

Andrea Lawlor

Len Lawson

Danielle Lazarin

Marcia LeBeau

Marie Myung-Ok Lee

Min Jin Lee

Wendy Lee

Stephanie Lehmann

Donna Levin

Edward Lewine

Stewart Lewis

Andrew Lewis Conn

Ed Lin

Kelly Link

Sara Lippman

Cari Luna

M

Martin MacKinnon

Octavia McBride-Ahebee

Emma McLaughlin

Charles McNair

Erika Meitner

Lynn Melnick

Jenny Bernard Merkowitz

Julie Metz

Jack Miller

Vica Miller

Anjali Mitter Duva

Rick Moody

Susan Muaddi Darraj

Meg Mullins

N

Scott Nadelson

Ann Napolitano

Christina Nelson Cook

Bailey Newman

Leigh Newman

Josh Neufeld

O

Dara O'Brien

Ted O'Connell

Stephen O'Connor

Greg Olear

Tim O'Mara

P

Stella Padnos-Shea

Fran Pado

Elizabeth Pagel-Hogan

Jonathan Papernick

Richard Peabody

Viktoria Peitchev

Sarah Pekkanen

Adam Penna

JT Petty

Helen Phillips

Arthur M. Phillips

Kala Pierson

Megan Pillow Davis

Nina Planck

Gae Polisner

Jennifer Probst

Q

Liz Queler

R

Emily Raboteau

Dawn Raffel

Joanna Rakoff

Austin Ratner

John Reed

Bushra Rehman

Hilary Reyl

Rahna Reiko Rizzuto

Christina Rice

Suzzy Roche

Josh Rolnick

Nelly Rosario

Liz Rosenberg

Lucinda Rosenfeld

Gabe Roth

Marco Roth

Jeffrey Rotter

Léna Roy

Domenica Ruta

Thad Rutkowski

S

Ami Sands Brodoff

Veronica Schanoes

Elissa Schappell

Amy Scheibe

Charlie Schulman

Helen Schulman

Mark Shulman

Christine Schutt

Ravi Shankar

Jessica Shattuck

Amy Shearn

Abby Sher

Rachel Sherman

Sarah Shey

Renee Simms

Robert Simonson

Karen Skolfield

Evan Smith

Amy Sohn

Anna Solomon

Matthew Specktor

Stephen Stark

René Steinke

Max Stephan

Darin Strauss

Terese Svoboda

Sheila Sweeney Higginson

T

Ben Tanzer

Chris Tarry

Whitney Terrell

Kristina Teschner

Erin Thompson

Matthew Thorburn

KC Trommer

Sergio Troncoso

U

Ellen Umansky

Daphne Uviller

V

Anjali Vaidya

Simon Van Booy

Laura Vanderkam

Orli Van Mourik

Susan Van Sciver

W

Raina Wallens

Helen Wan

Max Watman

Nicola Wheir

Diana Whitney

Kamy Wicoff

Ginny Wiehardt

Tia Williams

Lex Williford

Lauren Willig

Sari Wilson

Ronna Wineberg

Rebecca Wolff

Caeli Wolfson Widger

Y

Alicia Ybarbo

Marly Youmans

Z

Yona Zeldis McDonough

Alexi Zentner

Mary Ann Zoellner

Courtney Zoffness

Rachel Zucker

THE WRITER'S SNACK JAR

Testimonials
Pen Parentis Literary Salons

"It was a great program. You guys do such a great job. Onward!"

—John Freeman Gill

Author of The Gargoyle Hunters

"The discussions were lively and profound; the audience was so engaged. It was a great experience for me. I was impressed by the organization, too, by all Pen Parentis offers and the ways you encourage writers to keep writing despite the demands of parenting."

—Ronna Wineberg

Senior Fiction Editor, Bellevue Literary Review

Author, Nine Facts That Can Change Your Life

"Pen Parentis is a rare and invaluable resource for writers and other creatives who have children. While having children is of course enriching and an essential part of the life experience that writers seek to express, it's can also be an obstacle, in terms of networks and finances. Making the arts more sustainable to more people is a familiar mission statement, but Pen Parentis delivers."

—John Reed
Author of seven books including Snowball's Chance
Director of the Creative Writing MFA program at New School

"I loved every minute. You're doing a wonderful service to the writing and reading community and we all appreciate it!"

—Jamie Brenner
International Bestselling Author of 13 novels

"One of my first jobs in NY, in 1976 - was in a tiny office of a new organization called Poets & Writers. (There was some talk of calling it Writers & Poets.) I had a very important task-filling out index cards with writers' names and addresses for the new and bold concept of creating a writers' directory. The cards were expertly organized, alphabetically in shoe boxes. The only mention of mother/writers then was a debate over whether one could be a mother and a writer. Women often cited a long list of great women writers who never had kids...
This is a long way of saying thank you for last night. It was an honor to be part of it. I knew I would enjoy the evening with you guys, and it exceeded my expectations. Even made me want to get back to writing fiction."

—Patty Dann
New York magazine: Best Writing Teacher
Author of six books including Mermaids
(that the Cher movie was based on)

"*You have created something really amazing in the community, something unique and smart and supportive. It was an honor to be involved.*"

—Leigh Newman

"*It's so rare to speak at an event that has its own devoted following—and such a pleasure.*"

—Ellen Umansky

"*I loved reading at Pen Parentis! It was such fun and so inspiring!*"

—Myfanwy Collins

"*I want to thank you again for Pen Parentis, and for running such a great organization and reading series. Every time I have attended or participated, it has always been a lovely and inspiring evening, and this organization is so unique in its spirit of supporting writers.*"

—René Steinke
Author of Friendswood, Holy Skirts, and The Fires

"*Thank you for working to create this kind of support for parent-writers. It's an important need.*"

—Ginny Wiehardt
Poet

"To simply say thank you really doesn't cut it. I have felt in my own skin like an 'emerging writer' for close to twenty years; the recent salon at Pen Parentis, I experienced something rare and wonderful: a feeling of being valued. Of serving a useful purpose as a poet. I expect to always feel such gratitude to you."
Fondly,

— Stella Padnos-Shea
Poet
Brooklyn, NY

THE WRITER'S SNACK JAR

Testimonials
Pen Parentis Meetups

The 1st NYC Pen Parentis Writer-Parent Accountability Meetup Founded Summer, 2019

"Excited for a place to talk to people who understood my goals and dilemmas. I enjoyed the warmth and interest in my work and felt the suggestions were astute."

—Caitlin R., Meetup Participant

"Exciting to meet other writing parents! I needed the boost and encouragement."
—Burke G., Meetup Participant

"Excited to meet with other writers dealing with the same challenges and connect. It was great to chat with other writers about goals and writing with children."

—Teresa D., Meetup Participant

THE WRITER'S SNACK JAR

Testimonials
Pen Parentis Fellowship Responses

"I was so excited and grateful when I first heard about Pen Parentis – such a lovely and important community to be connected to."

—Becky Fine

Firesheets, Brooklyn, NY

"I was honestly thrilled when I first heard about Pen Parentis; it was so lovely to find an organization that sought to recognize and support writing parents and that seemed to understand what a challenge it is to do both."

—Megan Pillow Davis

2017-2018 Pen Parentis Writing Fellow - Louisville, KY

"Learning about Pen Parentis, I felt thankful to find a community of other writers trying to make it all work out, however messily."

—Thomas Fox

2017, his story "All Hallows' Eve" placed second in Fellowship decision - West Orange, NJ

"When I first heard about Pen Parentis, I felt thankful that an organization that helps writers who are taking care of small children existed. I knew that I wanted to be involved with it."

—Ledia X.

Fellowship Applicant - New York

"It felt like a breath of fresh air to meet the guidelines to participate in the writing fellowship. I appreciate this opportunity that recognizes parents that are authors and/or aspiring authors."

—Quisha H.

Fellowship Applicant - California

"What a joy to find Pen Parentis! You are the amplifier for the quiet (and often lonely) voice of the parent who writes."

—Candy B.

Fellowship Applicant - Wales

"As a parent, finding time to write is difficult. It's a great feeling to be challenging myself again, instead of just setting aside ideas for a later day, which may never come. Maybe there's a glimmer of hope for me to someday be holding the book that's lived in my head for years. Thank you for this opportunity."

—Danielle W.

Fellowship Applicant - Illinois

ABOUT THE AUTHOR

M.M. DeVoe was born to a traditional Lithuanian family of six in College Station, Texas. "M" was raised Catholic and bilingual by an organic chemistry researcher and a Montessori directress. She knows all there is to know about being an insider, an outcast, and an experiment. In college, she ran away with a group of jugglers who remain her best friends to this day. She earned her MFA at Columbia University as a Writing Fellow under Michael Cunningham and Helen Schulman. Her explorations of identity through creative writing have brought her to publish in nearly every genre: literary fiction, poetry, science fiction, urban fantasy, horror, even musical theater... she has won or been a finalist for more than 20 writing awards. She won her first grant for Pen Parentis from NYC's Department of Cultural Affairs in 2009 and remains its founding director to the current day.

ABOUT THE ILLUSTRATOR

June Gervais is a writer, artist, speaker, and cofounder of The MatriArtists, a cooperative circle of mama/artists. Her illustrated novel, Jobs for Girls with Artistic Flair— the story of a young woman chasing her dream of becoming a tattoo artist in 1980s working class Long Island—is forthcoming from Viking/Penguin (Pamela Dorman Books) in 2022. Find more of her work at junegervais.com and follow her on Instagram at @ the_matriartists and @june.gervais.writer.

ACKNOWLEDGEMENTS

Eternally grateful to:

Caroline Grant who knocked my socks off with a cross-country phone call and inaugural donation. Pen Parentis wouldn't be here if it were not for The Sustainable Arts Foundation.

Emily Speer Ryan & Michael del Castillo who willingly served on the first Board. Hats off.

Clive Burrow, The Gild Hall Hotel, and the Thompson Group for liftoff.

The team at Andaz Wall Street, the Killarney Rose, and Claire Rock at Westfield for letting us soar.

Jamie Clarke for sitting across the table and cheerfully picking up the pieces, from the very first salon to whatever comes next.

Lawrence De Voe, Loretta Shapiro, William Neal, Jenna Kalinsky, Darius Suziedelis, Lewis Gross, Michael Allen, Laura Rose (Larsen) Bloxham, Arlaina Tibensky, Denise Courter, Brian Gresko, and Emily Pulley who threw work and/or money and/or energy into the earliest stages of Pen Parentis. Thanks for your faith and encouragement.

Christina Chiu and Jackie McDougall who did more for this nonprofit than I can possibly relate.

Sonia de Beaufort, Mai Hoang, Tomas Paplauskas, Renee Simms, Marcia LeBeau, Brook Yimer, Lisette Boer, Caroline Willard, Vida Foubister, Marina Aris, Natalia Dymora, Aditi Davray, Renni Johnson, Helene Epstein, the team at Pace University led by Alan Krasner and headed by Jonathan Hill, the students at St. Edward's University, and all the Pen Parentis volunteer staff—you truly created the giving community that Pen Parentis espouses.

The fantastic Board and Title Members of Pen Parentis, past, present and future—you are all rock stars!

Mary Harpin for generously sharing her study for this book and for all her support.

And finally **Andrea Louie, Harry Precourt, Tracy Candido, Ben Francisco, Nick Kaufmann, Stuart Post, Jill Fine Mainelli, Rebecca Werner, and Tracy Kaufman** who taught me everything I know about being a proper arts leader.

If I left you out, it is because I haven't had my coffee yet. I will make it up to you in person, just DM me. I'm on Twitter @mmdevoe.

NOTES OF GRATITUDE

Thank You to Our Salon Curators

MM DeVoe with Christina Chiu
Salon Curator: 2015 — Present Day
Photo: Jenny Rubin

MM DeVoe with Brian Gresko
Salon Curator: 2013 — 2015

Thank You to Our Major Contributors

Washington College: Rose O'Neill Literary Center
Thank you for sponsoring our Pen Parentis Interns

**Seidenberg School of Computer Science &
Information Systems at Pace University**
*Thank you for developing the awesome
Pen Parentis Writer-Parent Mobile App*

Lower Manhattan Cultural Council

New York City Department of Cultural Affairs

Amazon Literary Partners

Amazon Smile Foundation

The Sustainable Arts Foundation

Poets & Writers

New York State Council on the Arts

WNYC/WQXR Radio Stations, NYC

New York State Council on the Arts
WNYC/WQXR radio stations, NYC

Thank You to Our Corporate Supporters & Partners

Paragraph: workspace for writers

LMHQ – NYC

Michael C. Allen and Co, CPAs

Tomas Paplauskas of **Web Solutions UAB**

Mutha Magazine

Empire State Center for the Book

Penguin/Random House

Literary Manhattan

Give Lively

Church Street School for Music & Art

Dreamers Creative Writing

brain, Child magazine

Bronius Motekaitis of **BCSWebstudio**

Thank You to Our Individual Sponsors

Emily Ann Pulley

Loretta Shapiro

Ellen Tepfer

Sergio Troncoso

Thank You for Reading

BOOK & BABY
The Complete Guide to Managing Chaos &
Becoming A Wildly Successful Writer-Parent

If you enjoyed this book, please consider leaving
a short review on Goodreads or your website of choice.

Reviews help both readers and writers.
They are an easy way to support good work and help to
encourage the continued release of quality content.

Connect with Milda M. DeVoe
www.mmdevoe.com

Want the latest from the Brooklyn Writers Press?
Browse our complete catalog.
www.brooklynwriterspress.com

BROOKLYN
WRITERS PRESS

CPSIA information can be obtained
at www.ICGtesting.com
Printed in the USA
LVHW030324090121
675851LV00005B/358